The View From Below

& Other Peerings

J.L. Fiol

authorHOUSE®

AuthorHouse™ UK Ltd.
500 Avebury Boulevard
Central Milton Keynes, MK9 2BE
www.authorhouse.co.uk
Phone: 08001974150

Published by AuthorHouse 04/18/13

ISBN: 978-1-4817-8992-9 (sc)
ISBN: 978-1-4817-8893-9 (e)

This book is printed on acid-free paper.

Because of the dynamic nature of the Internet, any web addresses or links contained in this
book may have changed since publication and may no longer be valid.

The views expressed in this work are solely those of the author and do not necessarily reflect the
views of the publisher, and the publisher hereby disclaims any responsibility for them.

For Family & Friends

The higher someone climbs up the ladder of fame, the harder the groundlings strain to catch a glimpse of bare arse.

J. L. Ruefull. *Seen from below*

Table of Contents

Foreword

A friend phoned to thank me for his copy of 'Second Coming … & other upheavals'. In reply to his question as to what I next intended to do, I said I'd wait and see what turned up. My friend then said that, knowing me, it would likely entail yet another sideways move, *like a crab*.

There and then, a vivid image of a crab changing into an ape, jumped into my head.

The result is the story 'The Crab goes Ape'. Then, with Gary the Crab having set the pace, here is another hotchpotch with scant regard for *Form* or *Genre*.

J.L.F. 2013

Cornwall

When You Dream

I'm good with dreams. I don't mean good good. What I mean is dreams are interesting and if you are interested in something you can get good at it.

In the Bible there was a man who was good at dreams as well and he had the same name as me.

If somebody came to me and said I've had this dream. There were seven skinny cows and they were coming out of the river what does it mean? I wouldn't say it means that there is going to be seven years when there is no food. You can't say that because it's in the future and the future hasn't happened yet. When the future is the present and then the past you can. It's called tenses. You have to do them in English grammar because I go to the Grammar school.

Here's one of my dreams. Listen to this.

I'm outside the gates of my school, right? All the Christian Brothers and the boys are inside and they are looking out. Then there's this noise and people screaming. A black horse is galloping down the hill to where my school is. When it's near I grab the reins and jump on its back where there isn't a saddle and it carries on galloping down the hill away from my school. The Christian Brothers and the boys go *ohhh* and they start clapping. We are going ever so fast. The black long hairs on the neck of the horse are flying in the wind. They are tickling my face and I am laughing very loud. But when we get to the bottom of Witham's Road I pull back the reins hard and the horse stands on its two back legs. I have to because there are people coming on Rosia Road towards us. It's a funeral. When I go to pat the horse to say it's alright the horse turns white. I go very sad and then I get angry.

Do you know what it means? I do. I worked it out because it's in the past.

I'm outside my school because I'm scared to go in. When the horse comes I can be scared of that instead. But it's less scary to jump on the horse than to run into the school and it looks braver anyway. That's why the teachers and the boys clap. It could have been a lion but I went to see My Friend Flicka in the pictures and there was a beautiful black stallion and you can't ride a lion. The funeral is coming because my granddad died in London when we were there when it was the war. Before that when I was four we had to go to Morocco because the war was coming and I used to go for walks with my granddad. One day we saw a procession with a Sultan and men playing music and soldiers carrying big swords. Best of all there were lots of white horses. My granddad said they were arabs. They were white with long black hair and their necks were like curves and they made breathing noises and walked like with little jumps. That's why the black horse turned white because when I saw the funeral I thought of my granddad when we saw the procession. I was sad because I loved my granddad and then I was angry because my grandmother said my granddad died because the night before I was cutting paper with a scissors and that's always bad luck. So that's what the dream means. Good ey?

This is what I think is really interesting about dreams. How come if you are asleep with your eyes shut and everything you can still see and hear and do things and go to different places.

The grown-ups say we all have five things called senses so we can see and listen and smell and taste food and touch things. I think there are more than five because sometimes I've heard them talk about the sense of fear and the sense of alone. There are others but I can't remember them … oh yeah … the sense of crustation. I'll probably find out when I'm a grown-up.

So all these senses can't work if we are asleep but in dreaming it's like when you are awake. And another thing. The dreams always tell a story. Not a story like in a book. It's sort of mixed up like in a code like spies use or hirolifics. That's writing with pictures like you find in the pyramids. You have to work it out.

If Bunny Ortega came to me and said Joseph I've had this dream can you work it out for me and in the dream Bunny was working in a circus because he was a clown and he kept tripping and the crowd clapped and laughed and he was happy I could work it out easily.

Bunny is twelve like me but he is smaller than me. I wear size four shoes but Bunny wears size eleven because he had to go to a Sanatorium and when he came out his chest and his neck were smaller but his feet were bigger. When he's doing Altar-serving Bunny keeps catching his feet and then he can trip and break sacred things, right? Now when he's a clown with those long shoes it's alright if he trips because it's his job and it makes people happy and Father Rapello hasn't got to tell him off and look grumpy. See? Simple.

The same with Palmero. Pretend that he has a dream that he's walking through a forest with trees and that he hears a noise and when he looks it's the wind and all the branches start swishing and hitting him. But when he wakes up in the dream it's not for real and it's not the trees hitting him it's a monster.

This is a difficult dream because it's like two dreams in one and Palmero cops it twice. What happens was that once when we were going home from school there was a Jeep coming and it went *Beeep* because we were mucking about on the road. Palmero said that's my uncle he's a soldier I'm going to stop him. So he got a branch and whacked the Jeep to stop his uncle. But when the Jeep stopped it wasn't his uncle so Palmero had to run away and hide in the bushes so the man wouldn't whack him. His dad did when Palmero got home late. Get it?

What about if Sampere had this dream that he was doing Altar-serving and the gregation kept laughing and when the Mass was finished and he went into the Sacristy to change and he looked in the big mirror he saw that he had a bare bottom because of this great hole in his cassock?

Do you know what that dream means if he had it?

It means that Sampere was very ashamed. It was his sisters' fault because they wanted a holy picture of Saint Francis of Sicily. So Sampere had to pinch one from the church and his sisters told on him. That would be very bad for Sampere because when he grows up he wants to be a priest but you have to be an Altar-server first and you can't with a hole in your cassock. Simple.

And what about Azzopardi. He's a funny one. What about if he said to me Joe can you help me with this dream and when he told me the dream was that he scratched Father Campbell with his long claws and his mum whacked him on the head with this comb so big she had to hold it with two hands?

Here's the answer to that dream.

When Father Campbell came to take the Masses in the week because Father Rapello had to go away he made the servers stand in a row because he was a militiry chaplin. Orfila said that was like Charlie Chaplin so we called him Padre Charlie. When the servers were in a row, Father Campbell looked at their hands because he said you couldn't touch holy things with dirty finger nails. When he came to Azzopardi Father Campbell said that's disgusting you've got fingers like sausages. That's because Azzopardi bites his finer nails right down. Azzopardi was angry because he said it in front of everybody. And then it was worse because Father Campbell said that all the servers had to have hair that was neat and tidy. But Azzopardi can't because he's got like a big mop of tiny black curls. It's his father's fault because he's Moroccan. His mum is Spanish and she's always saying that it's murder trying to get a comb through Azzopardi's hair.

So in the dream she has this massive comb so that she can do Azzopardi's hair but first she has to whack him with it because Azzopardi attacked Father Campbell with long claws. He had to because Azzopardi was very angry and you can't scratch anybody if you haven't got finger nails. Well it's true.

Martinez and me talk about dreams. He's interested in them as well. He says he wants to be an artist but it can be dangerous like with the chocolates. I don't tell him my dreams in case he can't understand them but he tells me his because he knows I'm good at them. Last week he had a bad one because he thought he had arithmetic but it was French.

In the dream there is a big black box. When Martinez opens it inside is Hapless Hassan and he is crying because the box is full of chocolates. Then Mr Robba comes in to take arithmetic but when he takes off his jacket it's the Groper. He is dressed all in black with very shiny long boots and he's got one of those bands with a sforsica on his arm. He looks different and he says to Hassan in a funny voice vot is zat. Hassan says nothing Sir it's not mine. Then the Groper says zen I vill haff it and when Hassan gets out of the box the Groper takes the box to his desk. Then when the boys are doing writing for French the Groper puts a chocolate in his mouth and he starts coughing and sneezing and spitting then a candle comes out of his mouth and his hair goes all funny.

That was a more difficult dream and Martinez was very worried in case the dream was about what was going to happen to him. I had to ask him lots of questions before I could get the answer. When I told him Martinez said *phew* and started to laugh and I did as well.

I'll explain the answer.

Martinez wants to be an artist, right? Azzopardi does drawings but he doesn't want to be an artist he says he does drawings to keep his dad from his back. He does the drawings with the charcoal he pinches from the church when he's doing Altar serving in Benediction. You use the charcoal to burn the incense. So Martinez can't do drawings in charcoal because if he takes charcoal as well Mr Bagu will find out and tell Father Rapello and then he'll have to go to Confession. Martinez not Mr Bagu. So Martinez still wants to be an artist, right? So he thinks you can still be an artist if you only do models. He gets the idea because he does models of cocks made into lollipops with sticks because his grandmother sells them and toffee apples. So he has this idea he can do models using the finished candles for the light at home. Then he starts collecting the wax from the finished candles in church. But one day he pinched two new candles because he was making important models. He took them from the grotto of the Virgin Mary of the inaccurate concession. He was making chocolates that looked like chocolates but of wax. Martinez told me they were brilliant and looked real because he mixed shoe polish with the wax to get the colour. But to make them even more real he wanted a proper chocolate box. So he asked Hapless Hassan to get an empty box of Black Magic chocolates from his dad's shop. He swapped it for a Stanley Matthews card because Hassan needed one for his collection. So Martinez takes in the chocolates to show Hassan and trick the other boys in arithmetic with Mr Robba. But instead of Mr Robba Brother Barratt came in to take French when Hassan was looking at the chocolates. The Groper had gone away somewhere to study when one of the boys punched him in French but now he was back. Martinez said he looked different and talked in a funny way. See in the dream the Groper comes in instead of Mr Robba, right? So Hapless is scared and hides in the box. The Groper has come back all strict like the Germans that's why he talks funny. He takes the box and when the class is doing writing from Marcel et Denise he puts a chocolate in his mouth but it's not made of chocolate so he starts coughing and sneezing and spitting. Then in the dream a candle comes out of his mouth. That's because Martinez pinched it and he's guilty. He has this bad dream because he's scared the Groper will tell the Lifter because he is the headmaster and he'll be in trouble. Martinez not the Lifter. So I said to Martinez the Lifter won't find out and he said how do you know. I told him because if the Groper said anything the Lifter would say why were you eating the chocolates. Martinez said that's right so he can't do nothing. So that's the dream … oh I nearly forgot. In the dream the Groper's hair looked all funny because the Groper wears a wig and when he was sneezing it sort of turned round. Great.

Sometimes dreams tell a story like in the opposite of what it is. Then you have to think what the true story is.

Like if Orfila had a dream about cushions and in it he was helping Mr Bagu to sit on one and then Father Rapello saw him and said how kind and then gave Orfila a glass of very red wine.

That would be the other way round because sometimes in Benediction Orfila hits Mr Bagu who is the Sacristan with one of those cushions you kneel on when they go behind the Altar. Another time Father Rapello called all the servers and he poured wine from a bottle in a glass and the wine was pink because Orfila drank the wine from the bottle and put water in it. In the bottle.

The same with Cabutto if he dreamed he was dancing all nice with the other boys and his dad saw him and said that's nice I'll buy you proper shoes for dancing and white trousers which are tight and then Cabutto was dancing on the stage and he couldn't lift the woman dancing on tiptoes with the little skirt and all the audience went *boo*.

That would also be the other way round because Cabutto is always fighting with the other boys and his dad has to whack him for fighting in school. Cabutto likes to come behind the boys and lift them up but the boys don't say anything because they're scared of him.

That's what I mean that dreams sometimes are the other way round.

One day when my father wasn't very angry he said to me so what are you going to do when you finish at the Grammar School with all those books. I said I would like to be a dreamist. He said what's that when it's at home. So I told him it's a job. Like a dentist but for dreams. He gave a nasty laugh and said now I've heard it all. But he hadn't. So I told him that you can study about dreams because when you dream you have your eyes shut because you are asleep but you can still see and everything. It's like there is like another one of you inside who can see and everything but in a different way. My father looked at the ceiling and then called my mother because she was peeling potatoes in the kitchen. When she came my father said to her here listen to this did you know we had two of idiot here one inside the other.

I didn't tell my father but also I think when grown-ups talk about Heaven that's about dreams as well. I don't think there's Hell. The priest tells you that so you can be good. But if you're good because you're frightened it doesn't count anyway. Also that babies are born with regional sin. How can that be true? Babies haven't done anything wrong you have to be older when you can go to Confession.

I think everybody goes to Heaven even when you do something bad. It's very difficult to explain because sometimes you know something is true but you don't know how you know. Sometimes if you do something bad it's not really bad because you didn't know or didn't mean it. Or you may live in another land and it's not bad there so you can't know until other people come and tell you. And then other people in other lands can think what you do is bad. So you can't always tell from the outside what is bad or good.

That's why I said to my father it's like there's another you inside. So it can tell. It's not really a person like you are a person. You don't know what it looks like or where it is in the body. It's probably next to the soul.

What I think happens is when you think and say and do things it all goes in there. Now the things that are good go to the soul because what's inside us can tell even if you are not very clever on the outside or you live in another land or are in a temper. The other things that are not yet good stay in that place until you are sorry or understand and then they go to the soul. Even if you are a saint the soul can't get full up.

Now when you die and go to Heaven I think this is what happens. Just before you die the soul sort of floats up or probably it just opens like flowers do and all the good things inside it go into your thoughts. Even if you die very suddenly like with an accident you still have time to think. If you were looking at your watch it wouldn't seem very long but it's in a different kind of time.

So you then close your eyes and begin to dream all the good things. Everything is very bright and clear. Then the people come to say hello. First all the people you love. Your family and your friends. Then other people. Some are famous. Everybody looks very beautiful. Not pretty or anything but because they are happy and shining because they can think and say and do all the good things they have always wanted. When you see your grandmother you don't have to say sorry because she understands.

So you keep dreaming finding more and more interesting things and more and more exciting things.

And the dream goes on for ever and ever.

Because you're dead.

So you can't wake up.

Azzopardi Loves Aeisha

Chipol found out and he told me. He lives in Lopez's Ramp and he saw Azzopardi going up to where Santos lives.

Azzopardi lives down in the town but he does altar serving in the Sacred Heart Church like me. That's why Chipol told me.

He said to Azzopardi where are you going and he said nowhere. So Chipol then said to him so why are you wearing wool gloves then and Azzopardi said because I'm cold. So why aren't you wearing a jacket Chipol said to him and he said because it's only my hands. Then Chipol noticed his hair and said to him what's wrong with your hair and Azzopardi said nothing. So Chipol said what have you put in it then and Azzopardi said it's only lard I've got to go and he went back down the steps.

In school I asked Azzopardi why he was going up Lopez's Ramp to where Santos lives. He said I never so I told him Chipol saw him. Then he got ever so worried and said please don't tell anybody promise you won't tell anybody. I said to him I can't promise because I don't know where you were going. So he said alright and he told me and then I promised. I didn't cross my fingers behind my back or nothing.

It was Aeisha. He said that when I told him about her in Benediction he went up Lopez's Ramp to see what she looked like. He said he went up three times but he couldn't talk to her only to look at her. He said she was very beautiful with long black hair with ribbons and a beautiful long dress with many colours and long gold earrings. He said when Chipol saw him he was definitely going to talk to her but then he couldn't. I said why were you wearing wool gloves and lard in your hair. He said because I wanted Aeisha to like me and if she saw my horrible hands and my hair all sticking up she wouldn't talk to me.

Then I remembered. It was Father Campbell's fault when he came for the weekday Mass because Father Rapello had to go away. He was a Military Chaplain so we called him Charlie like Charlie Chaplin. He made us stand in a row so he could see if we had clean finger nails. When he came to Azzopardi he said that's disgusting you've got fingers like sausages because Azzopardi bites his nails. And then it was even worse. Charlie said we all had to have hair that was combed neat and tidy. Azzopardi hates his hair. It's his father's fault because he is a Moroccan and Azzopardi has got like this huge mop with tiny little curls and his mum can't comb it.

It's true. I told Azzopardi about Aeisha but only because she comes from Algiers and he is half a

Moroccan because of his father. His mum is Spanish. Aeisha lives with her aunt and her uncle in the building where Santos lives because her mother and father went away. I don't like her uncle. Every time he sees me he looks at me all nasty like when you lower your eyebrows and twist your mouth. Like that.

On another day when we were in the playground Azzopardi said to me will you give this to Aeisha. It was a drawing made from charcoal because Azzopardi gets charcoal from the church. You use it to burn the incense for Benediction and the Mass on Sundays and for the processions. The drawing was of a face with long hair and also of hearts with names inside and arrows and writing. Azzopardi said the writing was a poem for Aeisha.

I told him I can't and he said why not I thought you were my friend. I said it was because of Santos and he said who's Santos and I had to tell him that he lives near Aeisha and he wants to be her boyfriend. Azzopardi said no he can't very loud and his face looked a bit like Aeisha's uncle.

It's true. One day in the summer holidays I went up to where Santos lives to go up the Rock with him. Aeisha was outside her door and said hello are you the boy who goes to the Grammar School so I said yes and she said I go to the Convent. I had to go for Santos but she kept on talking like isn't it a nice day and I like living here better than in Algiers and do you like going to the pictures and I do and do you take your girlfriend and I haven't got a boyfriend. Stuff like that. I couldn't say anything because I don't have girlfriends and anyway Santos was waiting for me. Then she said what do you want to be when you grow up so I said I didn't know. She said she was going to be a singer and she had a nice voice and did I want to hear it. I didn't know what to say so she started to sing. Not like Amapola and songs like that but like people sing in flamenco but it must have been in Algerian.

When Aeisha was singing Santos came out. He looked very angry. I thought because he had been waiting. I said shall we go and he said I'm not going anywhere with you clear off you little squirt. Because he's bigger than me. Then he made an ugly mouth and noises like snarling.

Another time we were outside his door with him. Me Chipol and Gomez. Then Aeisha came out and said hello and Santos said to me I can beat you at arm wrestling and grabbed my hand. So we started to wrestle standing up. I thought he was beating me but I held on and on and then all of a sudden Santos let go and he said his leg hurt and he had to go indoors. Chipol and Gomez started to laugh quietly and Aeisha was smiling.

After that it was really bad everytime Santos saw me. I couldn't understand it because we were friends. We went to the pictures together. We saw Destry Rides Again and Clouded Yellow and The Boy with Green Hair. Gomez told me that Aeisha told Santos to stop pestering her and that she liked me and Santos went mad and said when he saw me he would bash me.

That's why I didn't want to take Azzopardi's drawing and poem to give to Aeisha.

What happened after that was that Agius' Mum saw Azzopardi going up Lopez's Ramp lots of times and she said to his mum in church on Sunday what is your boy doing going up all the time up Lopez's Ramp where I live and Mrs Azzopardi said I'll find out.

So when she did she went to see Agius' mum and said to her do you know this girl. Agius' mum told him to go into the kitchen and shut the door but Agius kept it open a bit to listen because he knew about Aeisha.

Agius' mum said she knew the girl and when Mrs Azzopardi said what is her family like Agius' mum said not very nice and the girl is loose and comes from Algiers. So Mrs Azzopardi goes Holy Mother of God not from Algiers because Azzopardi's dad comes from Morocco. Then she said what am I going to do it's terrible and Agius' mum said I know I had the same trouble with the dollop in the kitchen I'll make some coffee. So Agius had to go quickly to pretend he was looking out from the window in the kitchen.

When his Mum made the coffee Agius said to her I'll hold the door open for you because he didn't want her to shut the door all the way. Mrs Azzopardi said this is nice coffee where did you get it and Agius' mum said it's Café La Negrita and she buys it in Granja's in beans.

Agius' mum said I noticed with the lump in the kitchen that he wasn't eating and he always eats like a pig. Agius said he nearly made a noise like a pig grunting. Then Mrs Azzopardi said what did you do and his mum said I did what you must do, do you want more coffee. Mrs Azzopardi said no thank you I'm too upset.

Mrs Agius said she went to see Doña Ludicra in La Linea and told her about Agius and the girl. The Doña woman said you did right to come because Algerians get up to all sorts and I can help you. She gave Mrs Agius a dead seahorse and said sew it in his jacket. If it doesn't work in two weeks come back and I'll give you something strong to put in his coffee.

So Mrs Azzopardi said did it work or did you have to go back for the stuff to put in the coffee. Agius' Mum said no because idiot in the kitchen thought it was a mouse and made a big hole and ruined a good jacket so his dad gave him what for and that was that.

Mrs Azzopardi said I wouldn't want Mr Azzopardi to give my boy what for and I'd be worried if he ruined his Grammar School blazer.

Mrs Aguis said you should go to Doña Ludicra but skip the seahorse and go for the drink straight away. Mrs Azzopardi said I will thank you for the coffee goodbye. Agius came out of the kitchen and his mum said have you been listening and he said how could I if I was looking out from the window.

When I saw Azzopardi again I said did you give Aeisha the drawing and the poem and he said nearly ever so miserable. He said he had stopped biting his nails and he was going to try again in two weeks. I said is it because of your hair and he said that as well but it's my mouth. He was talking funny like with his mouth shut but just opened a little bit in the corner. I said what's wrong with your mouth and he said his mum told him it was just growing pains and it would get better in two weeks. I don't believe that because I get very bad growing pains in my stomach and I'm not very tall and I have to drink tons of Camomile.

I said you don't have to talk to Aeisha just give her the drawing and the poem. He said I can't what if she sees it. I said sees what and he said sees this. Then he stuck out his tongue and it was bright blue.

The Crab Goes Ape

Last Saturday I saw Gary coming down the big steps. He's my friend, so I jumped down the small steps of my house and waited for him.

"Where are you going, Gary?" I said to him.

"I'm going to Marchena's and then to Carter's," he said to me all miserable because he had a red nose and was sniffing.

"Are you going to buy crickets at Marchena's?" I asked him.

"No" he said and sneezed. "Potatoes." Then he had to sneeze again.

It is the season and you can get crickets in Marchena's. He sells vegetables and fruits as well. He catches the crickets in San Roque where he lives and brings them in a big Oxo tin. He doesn't like selling the crickets. He gets all grumpy and says are you going to be all bloody day I've got customers waiting. It's because we want to see which are the best crickets for fighting and he's worried if they jump out of the tin. Once they all did and he said there is going to be bloody Hell to pay. He started chasing them but he's got this massive shoe you have to wear when you're lame and he squashed two and he didn't know why he bothered with the bloody things. Heh heh.

"I'm going to Granja's for a tin of Golden Syrup but first I'm going to Leo's," I said to Gary. "Shall we go together?"

"Oh alright," said Gary. So we started to walk along Lime Kiln Road together … well … not very together because Gary has to walk with his back to the wall. It's because of his trousers. He has a great big hole where his bottom is and he doesn't want people to see it. People call him Gary the crab because he walks like a crab. Sort of to one side.

He's got other trousers but they are for school. His mum is in hospital and his dad is always drunk and when Gary told him about the hole in his trousers his dad said you better mend it then.

When we got to Leo's I said to Gary you wait here by the wall. It was the house where Beppo lives. He is a big brown dog.

"What are you going to buy?" said Gary.

"A coconut square," I said. Coconut squares are new. They are brilliant and you get the cards with them now. They are made of square chocolate with coconut inside and silver paper on the outside. I keep it and make little silver cups with it like you win for sports. But smaller. I nearly won a cup on sports day. I came first in the obstacle race. But I didn't get a cup. I got a Sunday Missal and I already had one because I'm an Altar server.

Leo sells the coconut squares because he doesn't want to sell the cigarettes any more. You get six cigarettes in a yellow bag which is open and there's a card inside. The cigarettes are white with a red tip. You eat the red bit last.

When Leo kept the packets of cigarettes inside a box on the counter, we used to say can we have a penny bag of those sweets on the top shelf. Then when Leo got up on the ladder, we used to pinch the cards. Heh heh. So now when you buy a coconut square, Leo gives you a card from a drawer. The cards are of Famous Footballers, Soldiers of the King, Flags of the World, Famous Locomotives and Butterflies of the Amazon.

"This is the coconut square," I said to Gary when I got back.

"What's that?" he said and sneezed.

"It's a cigarette card" I told him. "You get them with coconut squares now."

"Oh" said Gary because he was wiping his nose and he didn't have a handkerchief. The card was No.13 Famous Locomotives The Flying Scotsman. I don't collect those but you can swap them. I collect Famous Footballers and Butterflies of the Amazon.

"Let's go halves," I said to Gary. I took off the silver paper and put it in my pocket and gave Gary half of the coconut square.

"Thanks," said Gary and ate his ever so quickly. I nibbled mine because I like to make shapes.

Then we had to cross over to the wall in Lime Kiln Ramp. There is no wall by Leo's because they are the steps that go up to the church and our school.

"See if there's the Priest or the Christian Brothers coming down," said Gary.

"All clear," I said. So Gary sneezed and ran to the wall in Lime Kiln Ramp and we went round the corner where Marchena's is in Castle Road.

"What are you going to buy when you get to Carter's?" I said to Gary.

"A tin of Camp Pie" he said.

"I better go to Granja's and get the Golden Syrup. My grandmother will be waiting to make the lollipops and toffee apples. Right. See you," I said.

"OK" said Gary.

* * * * * * * * *

Not yesterday the day before that I saw Gary again. He still had a red nose and he was sniffing but round one eye it was all black like with purple and green in it and it was shut.

"What happened?" I said to Gary.

"Nothing," he said all quiet.

"So who whacked you? Your dad?" I asked him.

"No," he said all mumbling.

"What then?" I said.

"I got into a fight," he said and sneezed.

"Who did you fight?" I said to him.

"Cabutto," said Gary all angry.

"Did he pick on you?" I asked him.

"No" said Gary. "I started it. I was angry and then I wasn't frightened and he ran away crying because his lip was bleeding," said Gary looking all pleased.

"Was it because he was calling you names like Gary the crab," I said.

"No. Not that," said Gary. "It was because of my trousers."

"How d'you mean?" I asked all puzzled.

"I got fed up with the hole in my trousers and people looking at me and walking by the walls so I mended the trousers." Gary said.

"What, you made a patch for it?" I asked him.

"No. I couldn't. The hole was too big and I couldn't find a cloth the same colour," he said.

I mended my trousers once. The grey ones. I was sliding down the scree behind the chicken runs and I tore them. So what I did was I made a patch. I cut off that bit that sticks out and you hook on to where your waist is. I used that. The trousers don't fall down or nothing because they've got buttons. I had to use white thread but when I finished I rubbed it with dust and it looked grey.

My grandmother never noticed but when I went to see my mother she said what's happened to your trousers. So I said nothing. Then she said where is that bit that sticks out and you hook on to where your waist is. So I said I dunno it must have dropped off.

"So how did you mend your trousers then?" I asked Gary.

"I had this idea," he said. "If I stitched lots and lots of thread over the hole like criss-cross, I could cover. So I said to Chipol and Agius and Gomez can you get me some thread from your mum because my mum is in hospital and I used that. But I needed lots so I had to use some of that thread you use for knitting and string from my kite."

"Did it look alright?" I said.

"Yeah, I think so" said Gary all pleased.

"What, all sorts of different colours?" I said.

"That's right," he said still pleased.

"Can I see it?" I said.

"No. You can't," he said. "I took it off."

"What, after Cabutto?" I asked.

"Yeah I told you," said Gary all angry again. "I whacked him. He was walking behind me laughing. And then he started yelling *what are you now Gary the crab … a baboon?*"

When Jacko Met Pancho

Brother Taylor said hang on and he put his hand on my shoulder. When all the other boys had gone out he said what have you been doing with yourself in the holiday trying to die?

I didn't know what to say so he said have you been ill? Then I said nosir. Then he looked at me and went *hmm* and said OK run around in the playground. I was going to anyway. Because I was feeling better.

He was wrong when he said have you been trying to die. Well he was a little bit right. Sometimes I feel like I didn't want to be born. Not all the time but it's worse when there is a holiday. I don't know why. It's not because there's anything bad or anything happening. Sometimes I feel like that even with good things. I don't tell anybody because I think it's what everybody feels sometimes. But Brother Taylor didn't say to any of the other boys have you been trying to die, so probably there is something wrong with me. But not ill. It's probably something I should tell Father Rapello in Confession in case it's like a sin. But it can't be a mortal sin because I don't mean it. It could be a venial sin but you don't have to confess those if you are not sure it's a sin.

There's this little grey monkey where the chicken runs are. It's got ever such a long tail. He's in this tiny cage with a chain round his waist. There's no room to climb. He just sits there with his hands inside his knees. Just looking. His eyes have got yellow rings and they don't blink. If you stand there looking at it even if it's for a long time it never looks back at you. It just looks straight in front. Like if it's thinking all the time. Probably about Africa.

If it's in the morning when I wake and it's not too bad but I know it's going to get worse I sometimes go up to the slopes and just climb and run till I get all sweaty and sometimes the bad feeling goes away. Then I can do things and play with the other boys. Football and that. If it's very bad I don't open the shutters or anything. I just sit in my room. Because then you can't move only breathe a little bit. My grandmother doesn't mind me staying indoors because she knows where I am and not getting up to all sorts and getting hurt.

If I'm doing something interesting or something exciting happens or if one of my friends comes for me to play or go to the pictures or something then sometimes I feel OK. But not if it's really bad. Then I have to pretend.

Once I was climbing up to the railings up from the first tower. Then in front of my face there was this big *lagarto*. It's a big green lizard. Its mouth was open all red with lots of little white teeth. It must have been scared as well because it dived into a hole in the rock. They stand still like that with the mouth open to get warm in the sun because then they can move better.

I'd love to catch a big one like that and keep it or take it to the new museum. The men say if you want to catch a lagarto you have to wear a straw hat. What you do is you take your hat off and let the lagarto bite it. Then its teeth get caught and you can grab it. I never wear a hat. Ever.

I catch small lizards and I'm very good at catching geckos. They are brown and grey so it's hard to see them. I catch them in Alameda Gardens when I am going home from school with my friends. Suddenly I say to them don't move there's a gecko. They say how can you see them so far away. Well there are these walls with holes in them. The walls hold up the earth which goes up in steps. The holes are for the water to run out when it rains or the wall and the earth fall down. Now, these holes are sort of square and they are dark right? The geckos come a little bit out of the holes to get the sun. I don't really see the geckos when it's far. What I see is a different pattern in the holes because they aren't square – so I know it's a gecko.

To catch them you have to get near very slowly. You have to go from behind them because then they can't see you because their eyes are on the sides of their heads. Then when you are close you grab them ever so fast. You have to be careful you don't squash them. Sometimes a bit of the tail comes off and they get away. But it doesn't hurt them and it grows back again.

It's different if you want to catch a fly. They have eyes all round and they can see everywhere. So what you do is you come close very slowly. What you have to do then is guess where the fly will go when it sees your hand coming and grab there. It's the same with goalkeepers when they have to stop a penalty kick. They can't wait till the centre-forward kicks the ball because it goes too fast because it's near. What the goalkeeper has to do is guess where the ball is going to go and dive there. It doesn't work all the time. Like with the flies.

Sometimes if you are scared of something or if something scary happens, you can feel better after. It's because if you are feeling scared you want to run away and then you can do things. It's what happened one day when I was going up to the slopes when I knew it was going to be bad. When I got to where Mr Victory's chicken-run is I stopped.

The apes were coming down along the wall next to the houses. Pancho came out of his kennel and started to bark on the flat roof of his house opposite to where the chicken-run is. Pancho is a Bull Terror dog. He's big and white and he's got a big ugly head with pink eyes. He barks at everything but worst of all the apes. Gomez said that in the old days they mixed a dog with a bull and that's how you got the Bull Terrors. Gomez knows about dogs because he had a dog called Rocky but it got rabies.

The apes were very near and Pancho started to growl and bark louder. Then the apes stopped on the wall opposite to Pancho and started making monkey noises and screaming at Pancho. I was scared to move in case the apes saw me and came to attack. They do sometimes if they think you've got food and won't give it to them. Ever so slowly I hid behind a wall made with those flowers called Morning Glory by Mr Victory's gate and watched through the leaves.

The noise was terrible. All the apes got excited and screamed and fought with each other and threw stones at Pancho. He was going mad and nearly fell from the flat roof to get at the apes. Then in the middle of all the noise there was this screech *chatachatatak*. The apes stopped fighting and screaming only Pancho carried on but more quietly.

Then this huge ape came down along the wall slow and quiet. It was Jacko. He's the leader of the apes. He stopped and made another noise *chatachiktak* and all the apes started to go back to the slopes. Jacko waited till they all went. First the mothers with the babies and then the old apes and last the young ones and then Jacko went and sat on the wall opposite to where Pancho was.

Pancho wasn't barking. He was making a low growling noise like in the throat. Jacko got up and then he jumped. It was marvellous like in slow motion in the films. He stretched out his arms like he was flying and landed on the drainpipe of Pancho's house. Then he climbed up the drainpipe sort of slow and strong like King Kong when he climbed up the skyscraper.

He got to the top. Pancho went all quiet and walked backward a bit. Jacko got up on the flat roof and sat down. Pancho put his head down and showed his huge teeth and his tail was all stiff. Jacko just sat there but he did not look at Pancho. Then he stood up slowly and looked at Pancho.

I thought this is it. Like King Kong and the dinosaur. They're going to fight to the death. Pancho walked towards Jacko. In a funny way with his back legs all stiff. Jacko stood still just looking straight at Pancho's face. Pancho stopped close to Jacko then lifted his head like he was sniffing. Still Jacko didn't move.

Then a strange thing happened. Pancho lay down and crossed his paws in front of him. Then he put his head on his paws and made a sound like a little laugh and made a little wag with his tail. Jacko walked slowly past him to where the kennel was. He picked something from a red bowl then came back and sat in front of Pancho again. Then Jacko was eating something but I couldn't see what it was and Pancho lifted his head and wagged his tail again.

Both of them got up and nearly touched noses. Pancho went back to his kennel. Jacko climbed down the drainpipe. He walked round the wall and came past where I was hiding and carried on walking on the steps up to the slopes.

I didn't carry on walking up to the slopes. I was feeling excited and went down back home. I got canes, tissue papers in different colours, string and mixed flour with water to make a kite. Next morning I took it up to the slopes by the first tower and flew it ever so high.

The Stump and the Strongbone

When people say to Mr Felipe why don't you put a rubber tip on your leg, he tells them it's because of the music.

He has a wooden leg but it doesn't look like a real leg and he keeps the trousers rolled up. You know if you got a coconut shell and cut it in half and then put a piece of broomstick on it and put your knee inside? It looks like that. Like Long John Silver. Also it looks like one of those things you use if the sink gets blocked. If Mr Felipe's wooden leg got broken, he could put his knee in one of those till he mended it.

When he walks on the road the leg goes *clunk clunk*. But if he walks on the pavement it goes *clack clack*.

He lives near me and sometimes I can hear him playing his flute. He plays *Amapola* and *Ojos Verdes* and other songs. I know how they go but I don't know the names. When it's night-time and it's very quiet and you can smell the night flowers it sounds very nice. He says he's not keen on church music but what can you do, you've got to eat.

I don't like church music either but I'm in the choir. The words are worse than the music. Plain chant is the worst. It's what monks sing. We call it *pain* chant. Brother Alleluia said plain chant is easy. All you have to do is go up when the square dots go up and go down when they go down. When I said how do you know how high to go and how low to go, he gave me a shove on the head and said stop picking nits. High is high and low is low.

I like George Formby. He sings funny. We play it on a record on Gomez's gramophone. It's like a cupboard and you turn a handle. The record has *Mr Wu's a window cleaner now* and *when I'm cleaning windows* and *my granddad's flannelette night shirt* and *my little stick of Blackpool rock*. The best bit is when George Formby plays the banjo at the end of the songs. *Taka-taka-taka-taka-ta*. Brilliant.

Mr Felipe has a band. It's only a small one but he is the leader. What he does is when they are playing marching or standing still he plays his flute and he keeps time with his stump. *Clunk clunk clunk*. Not *clack clack clack* because they don't play on the pavements. He doesn't mind playing for the Cathedral because there it's flat. But near the Sacred Heart Church where we live it's very steep. Mr Felipe says it can be murder. He says it's better to play a slow hymn when you are going up the hill and a quick one when you go down.

* * * * * * * * *

Don Alonso also has a band but it's a bigger one. He hasn't got a wooden leg but he's got wooden feet. Lots of them. He uses them for when he makes shoes because he's a shoemaker as well as the leader of a band. *Ha ha*.

He plays the *strongbone* and he waves it to keep time when he's playing it. He doesn't like playing and marching at the same time. He likes to play a bit and then march a bit. When they are marching Mr Fortuna keeps time with his drum. *Boom boom boom*. It's alright when it's flat. When it isn't Mr Fortuna gets into trouble. Sometimes when it's flat as well because Mr Fortuna has a huge drum and he's not very tall so he can't see over the top of it. Once Mr Suarez who was marching in front said to him *bump me one more time and see what happens*. Going downhill is bad. Mr Fortuna has to lean back and he's not very thin so the drum is a long way in front of him and he hasn't got very long arms so he sometimes hits the metal bit round the drum and it doesn't go *boom boom*. Then Don Alonso swears at him and then tells him *can't you keep bloody time*. Going uphill is bad as well. He has to lean forward. He can reach better but the drum bumps on the ground and Don Alonso has to swear at him again.

Don Alonso hates church music. He says it sounds like someone trying to go to the toilet. He told Father Rapello before he left why don't we play proper music like in Opera. But Father Rapello said the Bishop couldn't wear it. And then Don Alonso said to Father Rapello don't talk to me about Felipe and his band. You can't call that a band with a cripple and no drum. What sort of band is it with idiots playing mouth organs. That's for idiots who can't understand music. Proper music.

* * * * * * * * *

It was Father Donohue's fault. But he didn't know because he is a *navel chaplin* from HMS Rooke. He came to take the Mass in the week after Father Campbell. He is a *militiry chaplin* from the army and he came because Father Rapello had to go away to pray.

We called Father Campbell Charlie because of Charlie Chaplin. So we couldn't call Father Donohue that even if he was a chaplin as well. So we called him Stan. He wasn't fat and with a moustache so we couldn't call him Oliver.

Father Stan was not grumpy like Father Charlie. He was always happy and smiling. Mr Bagu who is the *Sacrosant* says it got on your nerves because you didn't know what the blessed man was thinking, at least with Father Rapello you knew where you were standing.

This is what happened. Father Stan said we should have a procession, one of our own the Cathedral's got one. That's right. It's called the Corpus Christi. That means the Body of Christ in Latin. But they don't carry a statue of Jesus in the procession only of his Mother because the Cathedral is called St Mary the Crowned.

The Corpus Christi is when you are confirmed. I was confirmed. It was terrible. You had to wear this shirt like girls have all white with bits and a ribbon round your head. And on your arm you had this big bow with letters made of gold. And socks you had to keep up with elastic. And very shiny black shoes. And God help you if you got them scratched. I was scared the night before because Cabutto said the Bishop had to slap you on the face when he was confirming you. He could only use two fingers but it had to be hard. Because you had to be tough when they make you a soldier of Christ. The procession was terrible. You had to go all along Main Street. There was a big crowd. Some people only go to laugh at you and see if your socks fall down.

Father said that in our procession we should carry the statue of the Sacred Heart because that's the name of our church. I know the statue. It's of Jesus pointing to a hole in his chest where His Heart is. The Heart looks like it's burning. It's a big statue.

Father also said we should have lots of music because it makes people happy and takes them together. Mr Bagu had to tell Mr Spiteri because he is a knight of St Columba and he likes to be in charge. Mr Spiteri said what music from the choir? Mr Bagu said no from a band. Mr Spiteri told Mr Bagu didn't you tell him about last time. Mr Bagu said how could I he wouldn't listen he just kept smiling. Mr Spiteri said we had a right one here still it's his funeral and you know how mad Father Rapello went. Mr Bagu said his hands were tied.

That's right. I remember. Father Rapello was furious because he knows Spanish. Mrs Stagnetto who does the flowers said you couldn't go near him afterwards because he was fit and could burst.

So Father Stan went to see Don Alonso to play the music for the procession. Don Alonso told him no can do my boys can't wear it. We don't do marching and playing at the same time have you tried doing it up those hills. Father Stan said he hadn't but was there a way round it. Don Alonso said why don't you ask Long John Silver. Father Stan said who's he. Don Alonso said it's that peg leg Felipe. He's got a band if you can call it that with idiots playing the mouth organ and no drum. Father said I'll go and see this Mr Felipe. What about if your boys stay in the church yard and when the other band is coming back playing to the church your boys can join in and it will be wonderful. Don Alonso said he would put it to the boys but he couldn't make promises.

Then Father Stan went to see Mr Felipe and he said he wasn't keen on church music or going up and down those hills but you've got to eat haven't you.

* * * * * * * * *

When it was the day of the procession I went to the church early to change into an Altar server because I was in the procession. There was already a crowd in Lime Kiln Steps. Leo's shop was open and the grown-ups were buying sweets to keep the children quiet.

When it was nearly time to start the men had to take the statue of the Sacred Heart out to the church yard. It's very hard work but the men like to do it because you get a *pinery pridulgness*. What it means is when you die it counts for Heaven.

The statue wouldn't go through the church door because of the cart with the long poles that the men carry on their shoulders. They had to take off a piece of wood and then it did. The pillars in front of the church were difficult as well. Mrs Stagnetto took off some of the flowers in case they got squashed.

The worst thing was the three steps going down to the church yard. The men were swearing and shouting and puffing. *Steady … no back a bit … a bit forward now … no no hold it.* Agius' big brother started shouting at Mr Porro *lift your end … more … more … are you deaf.* Mr Porro shouted back *no you have to drop your end … I haven't got telescopes in my arms … and don't take that tone to me you little squirt I remember you when you had a snotty nose.*

The statue went all wobbly and started to fall forward and the crowd went *oooOOh*, then it went straight and everybody clapped and cheered.

So then we were ready to start and we had to get in line. First it was Mr Felipe and his band behind him. Then Mr Bagu carrying the long silver crucifix, then all the Altar servers. After us it was the statue of the Sacred Heart with the long poles and the men. Then Orfila swinging the incense. Then Father Stan like under a tent with silver poles carrying the *monstrous*. It's what you use for Benediction. It's made of gold like with the rays of the sun and in the middle is the Sacred Host. Then last of all all the good Catholics.

Father Stan gave a little nod to Mr Spiteri and he went *pheeeep* with his whistle like referees have for football. Everybody went dead quiet. There was only a dog barking. Then Mr Felipe went *clack clack clack* and the procession started to move out of the church gates.

We then made the line again on the top of Lime Kiln Ramp. Mr Spiteri blew his whistle again and Mr Felipe went *clunk clunk clunk* this time. The band started to play and we all went down Lime Kiln Ramp quickly because it's very steep singing *what a friend we have in Jesus*. When we started to climb up Castle Road we went more slowly. People were looking from windows and standing on the road.

When we went past the Police Barracks we stopped where there is some level road at the bottom of Williss' Road where it gets really steep. It's where the mules have their stable. We said lots of prayers and the Litany and Father Stan made a sermon. It was called *those who toil for the Lord*. It went on a long time and he kept smiling all the time. Then we had to sing *Inaccurate* Mary and Faith of our Fathers and Panis Angelicus. Then Father Stan gave a blessing with the *monstrous* and we all made the sign of the cross amen.

Father gave another nod and Mr Spiteri gave another whistle. *Clunk clunk clunk.* Down Castle Road we went quickly and stopped at the bottom of Lime Kiln Ramp on the way back to the church.

The band started to play again ever so slow and sad. We started to sing and went up Lime Kiln Ramp ever so slow. The hymn was the old Rugged Cross. *Waah-waah-waah-wah-wah-waaaah.* People were singing from the windows and the street. Some of the old women were crying.

When we were getting near the top where the church gate is, you could see there was a big crowd by Leo's waiting for the procession. They all crossed themselves when we went past. Then they followed us into the church yard. It was very crowded. Don Alonso was there with his band.

Mr Felipe was still playing the old Rugged Cross with his band and people were still singing. Then Don Alonso raised his *strongbone* and … *boom boom boom* and his band began to play. *Taa-ra-ra-raa-raa-ra-ra-raa-ra-raaah.*

It wasn't the Old Rugged Cross. Mr Felipe's band stopped playing and the people stopped singing. Don Alonso's band was ever so loud.

Then people started to sing again ever so softly. And then louder and louder. Some of the men put their fist up in the air. Father Stan was all happy and smiling because he doesn't know Spanish and he thought the people were singing a catholic hymn in Spanish.

It wasn't. What everybody was singing is called *In the nasty alley*. It's what the conomist sing.

It starts *cara al sol con la camisa nueva, los calzoncillos remenda'o.* That means *stand up and face the sun with the new shirt and the underpants with patches.*

Then it gets a bit more rude and when the people were singing they were laughing behind their faces. *Ha ha ha.*

Passion Fruit & Veg

Maruja leans forward to the wardrobe mirror. She makes a sideways pout. A little finger deftly wipes a smear of red from the corner of her mouth. A dampened middle finger traces the arches of both eyebrows.

She straightens. Practised hands scrunch flick tease and twirl the tumult of raven hair cascading onto her shoulders. Large gold ring-earrings take up their position. Hooked thumbs pull down on décolletage to expose further sun-mellowed swell. Smoothing hands slide down from the overhang to waist, over stomach and around hips to buttocks. The dress, the blood red of her lips, fits with a tightness well able to faithfully describe the undulations of her generous contours.

She goes over to the window and looks down. She waits. The last of the squat black-clothed customers trundles homeward. Maruja hurries out of the room and down the main stairway, her high heels castanets on stone. At street level she stops for brief final adjustments before starting to slowly walk with gentle sway towards the tethered donkey.

The vendor is busily rearranging, with scowling ill grace, the scatter in the panniers from the probing and prodding of the departed clientele. Seeing Maruja approaching, he faces her with hands on hips. With one finger he tips back his hat in cowboy fashion and does repair work on the scowl to show the gold canine to advantage.

"Beginning to think you didn't want anything today," he calls out.

"Ah, missing me, were you?" says Maruja with mock pity as she draws near. "See what you've got today." She goes over to the panniers and makes a show of leaning over them, sufficient to nail the eyes of the vendor.

"What are the melons like today?" she enquires conversationally. The donkey twitches an ear and stamps a back hoof.

"Ay ay ay, madre mía," laments the vendor, entering into the initial stage of his torment, his top lip beginning to glisten. "Sweet definitely sweet. Sweet and ripe," he says in reply.

"Your cucumbers don't look up to much," she observes in the tone of a discerning shopper. She picks up with two fingers a twisted specimen, shrivelled and warty.

"How about this one?" helpfully suggests the tradesman fishing an alternative example of Cucumis Sativus, rampant in rectitude.

"More like it," demures the customer under her breath. The donkey gives a rolling snort. "Right" continues Maruja in brisk shopping mode. "Let me see now." The vendor's eyes cloud over at the inevitable, as he prepares to set aside the items of Maruja's choice.

"Oh yes. I'll have two aubergines; three lemons; grapes if they are seedless; potatoes of course; carrots; onions; spinach; small cauliflower; celery; runner beans; courgettes; tomatoes; the lettuce looks a bit sorry for itself I'll leave it; oh parsley; flat; garlic several large ones; the cucumber I've got; pumpkin only a quarter; are those medlars, I love them, quite a few; figs the black ones; Jaffas better make it six; peppers red and green no yellow; what are those under the leaves, mulberries, definitely some, it's only a short season; now, have I forgotten anything?"

"Wouldn't think so," mutters the vendor wearily.

"No. Can't think of anything else," muses Maruja quite unperturbed. "Unless you've got something special tucked away." The donkey whinnies.

The vendor stares mutely at the pile, numbed by the conflict raging within: the male in the vendor and the vendor in the male at war.

"Well, you better tell me what this little lot comes to" says the shopper with resigned breeziness. The vendor doesn't stir. He waits. "Oh no" exclaims Maruja aghast, looking around. "Would you credit it? I've only gone and come down without my purse … and my bag." The vendor waits. "Honestly, I'd forget my head if it wasn't … *screwed* … on." The donkey's own head droops. "Would you be a dear and bring the stuff up for me. Save my legs. I'll … *settle* … with you upstairs. The donkey gives a stifled bray.

While Maruja looks on smiling sweetly, the vendor loads his wide raffia basket. He hefts it off the panniers and with a breathy groan, grasps it to his chest. He waits for Maruja to lead the way and then follows her at an appropriate tradesman's distance.

Up the stairway they go, the distance between them lessening. The vendor in an agony of anticipation transfixed by the motion of the dress and contents: now tensing, now softening. He stumbles twice, falling forward. The onerous basket on both occasions moonlighting from impediment to cushion against injury.

At the summit Maruja stands in the doorway making his entry a test of character.

"Where do you want it?" he enquires with a candour which belies double-entendre.

"I should have thought you knew that by now," retorts the relentless Maruja. "Oh, the bag … make room on the sideboard." Relieved of physical burden, the vendor goes to the window and looks down anxiously. Maruja kicks off her shoes and approaching him with stealth, fondles the back of his neck. From above the donkey presents as an outlandish moth with the produce in the panniers providing colourful wings.

"Your mind still on your work?" purrs Maruja. The battle between the male and the vendor is at climax. The vendor turns. A little despairing sob escapes. He plunges his face into the sun-mellowed swells, carried in the bliss of infant recollection.

"Ohhh" he articulates surfacing as might a seafarer in sight of land. One hand seeks purchase on the drum-skin dress. The other attends to personal preparation.

Maruja's hands rest lightly on the quivering shoulders. Her eyes are turned to the street below, the line of her eyebrows quizzical her demeanour distant with rueful amusement.

"Oh, oh." Thwarted and unaided, his own preparation complete, the vendor accelerates into a more haste less speed condition, both hands made claws by the desperation of frustration.

"Oh," says Maruja. "Look."

"Ohh ohh … huh?" from the vendor, squeezing irritation from his involvement.

"Look," repeats Maruja, indicating with a nod.

"Aaagh," explodes the vendor.

* * * * * * * * *

"Wot, every day?"

"No-o. He only comes to my street on Thursdays."

"Wot, after school?"

"No. In the morning."

"So how do you know? We are in school then."

"Not in the holidays."

"Do they do it?"

"Ellul says they do."

"How does he know?"

"Because he lives below her."

"So how can he see them?"

"He hears them. He says they make a lot of noise."

"What sort of noise?"

"Like when you're hurt."

"They are probably not doing it. Only fighting."

"So who was there?"

"Me, Borastero, Ellul, Torres and Pardo."

"Did you all get something?"

"Yeah."

"What did you get?"

"Grapes but they didn't have any pips. I like the pips. You can spit them out like a pea-shooter. Borastero got the most. Figs, oranges and apples. He dropped an orange and it rolled all the way down the hill. Pardo got mulberries and it made his hands purple and it wouldn't come off. Heh heh. He said I'm in for it now."

"Heh heh heh."

"Guess what Ellul got."

"I dunno."

"Potatoes and a cabbage."

"What for?"

"To help his mum because she's not well. And you know Torres?"

"Yeah, wot?"

"He was scared. He didn't want to get nothing. He said what if the man comes. Borastero said he won't come. He'll be a long time, Ellul said. You know what he got? A carrot."

"Why?"

"Because the man came out running and shouting. So Torres got anything and we all scarpered."

"Was he very angry?"

"Who Torres?"

"No. The man."

"Oh yeah. All red and swearing as well."

"Did he catch anyone?"

"Nah. He kept having to stop because of his trousers."

Exceptions: 1

The Pen is mightier than the Sword.

EXCEPT

If goading an enraged Samurai with a Biro.

Exceptions: 2

Do unto others as you would others do unto you.

EXCEPT

If you practise Sado-Masochism

003½

The taxi backs on to the front. 19.04. 4 minutes late. I pull the grille to. Snap the padlock. Walk up to the driver. Tap my watch. Traffic, he says. I jump in the back.

Out of Secretary's Lane. Past the Cathedral. On to Bomb House Lane. Clear run. Pick up Glacis Road. Hold-ups. 19.18. A gap. The driver looks in the mirror. I nod. He hits the pedal. The barrier not down. Speed across the runway. Park. 19.23. We wait.

A rush of wind. BEA Flight 1956 from the UK. 7 minutes delay. Drive on to the tarmac. Passengers get off.

He's the last. I run up the steps. Show my ID. He nods. We make the handover. 4, I say. Correct, he says. We get into the car. Duty Inspector salutes. Waves us on. We go past Passport Control. Past Customs. Diplomatic privilege. Arrive back at the Secretariat. 20.17.

That's pretty much how I half-envisaged my contact with the Queen's Messenger: the 'drops'; the 'pick-ups'. Well … I was barely twenty-two. A bit 007. In reality it was more Tinker Tailor Soldier Spy. Not that I'd heard of either Bond or Smiley at the time. Now, after more than fifty years, I incline to the flavour of Tinker Tailor: the seedy quiet despair of disillusionment; the faceless trudge. Far more interesting than the uncomplicated physicality and self-assured resources of Mr Fleming's creation.

I daresay, in fairness to Mr Fleming, that were I able to work up sufficient interest to delve into the original qualities of Bond, I might well find it hard to credit the pumping up which has gone into the marketing of the Brand: the embellishment necessary in transferring the paper of the books to the celluloid of the films. In the latter, the focus appears concentrated on image with content largely relegated to ever-escalating special effects.

The favoured image is one of suave unruffled sophistication. Always a 'cut-above' and not just sartorially. Seductive with libido to match. Of exquisite, if jaded, fastidiousness.

Bond. James Bond. Martini. Shaken. Not stirred. Wow.

Ramsbottom. Clive Ramsbottom. Lager. Straight glass. Perhaps not.

Were it conceivable for Bond to have a penchant for toast, surely it could only be accommodated by reference to the specifics of a colour chart.

Then there's the inherent superiority of British sang-froid, in marked contrast to the frantic floundering of Johnny Foreigner in the face of the impending. The savoir-faire indolence of the fronted lounge lizard, able to instantly galvanise at the behest of world Governments as the only hope of averting cataclysms.

Based on my little knowledge of the Principle of Action and Reaction as well as of the less formulated laws of natural compensation, I fear for the persona of Bond.

That level of control in mastering situations and also personal responses; that icy appraisal and resolution regardless of peril; that sexual potency on orthodox lines cannot be indefinitely sustained and need sometimes to relent.

I can only hope that it doesn't periodically manifest in submission, black-rubber clad, to the whip of a dominatrix or alternatively in regression to nappy-clad helpless babyhood.

Perhaps my fears are groundless and Mr Fleming's construct is impervious to any such laws and my suggestion to the contrary simply a reaction to the lingering taste of sour grapes.

* * * * * * * * *

"How long have you been with us now, Foster?" As he spoke, Mr Brevitt's concentration was directed at filling his pipe.

"Foyle Sir," I corrected apologetically.

"That's right. Foyle," conceded Mr Brevitt, between determined sucking sounds and spurts of fire. "How long did you say?"

"I didn … over five years, Sir."

"Capital." He gave a little contented grunt, which I took to be directed at the state of ignition rather than at my impressive length of service. He then proceeded to engulf himself in a bluish fug which, catching a stray shaft of sunlight, rendered him ethereal. I waited for him to regain substance. On emerging, he favoured me with an earnest little nod.

"I've been hearing good reports, Fos … er …Foyle."

"Thank you Sir." I effected a fleeting grimace intended to convey humble embarrassment.

"Keen on caving, are you?" continued Mr Brevitt straining towards bonhomie.

"A bit Sir," I parried warily.

"Capital." Mr Brevitt allowed himself three vigorous puffs. He leaned forward with elbows resting on the pristine green blotter with brown leather corners. "How would you feel about a spot of special duty, eh?" The tone veered between enticing and conspiratorial.

"Alright Sir" I answered on *orange alert*. There was bound to be a snag. Ramagge sprang to mind.

We did National Service in the same Intake. One day the Battery Sergeant-Major stomped into our hut and asked if any of us rookies could play the piano, whereupon Ramagge sensing special duties and a cushy number, promptly raised his hand. The BSM then requested Ramagge to report on the double to the Quartermaster. A piano needed shifting. Ramagge landed himself an inguinal hernia.

"Heard of the Queen's Messenger, Foster?" continued Mr Brevitt, reverting to type.

"Yessir," I replied cautiously. "He travels carrying classified documents in diplomatic bags, Sir."

"That's the ticket" assented Mr Brevitt, visibly relieved by not having to explain further. "Thing is we're in a bit of a fix. There's been a bit of a hitch and your name came up." Then in the voice of one handing out a diploma, he said: "You may be just the chap for the job."

"Job Sir," I postulated, upgrading to *red alert*.

"You know. Meeting the QM at the airport. Taking charge of the diplomatic bags. Seeing to the paper work. That sort of thing. Be out of office hours, working on your own initiative. No overtime remuneration entitlement, I'm afraid."

"I understand Sir," I said, fully au fait with the conditions of employment in Her Majesty's Civil Service.

"Well, what do you say, Foster?" queried Mr Brevitt beaming expectantly.

"I'll give it a go Sir," I acquiesced dropping to *yellow alert*. The airport thing appealed to me. I'd never met a plane.

"Capital," said Mr Brevitt in a tone of *mission accomplished*. "I'll put you in touch with the CMO."

"CMO Sir?" I remonstrated, firmly back on *red alert*. In the course of my ascribed duties as Despatch Clerk, Clerical Grade 1 Permanent and Pensionable, CMO stood for Chief Medical Officer.

"Classified Material Office, Foster," half-snapped Mr Brevitt. "Branch of the DSO. You'll need to be briefed." I knew about the DSO: Defence Security Office. I sometimes rang one of the departments about routine security clearance in applications for British Nationality.

* * * * * * * * *

The taxi purred in reverse down the narrow lane to where I waited. I dragged the heavy grille to the main entrance shut and snapped the padlock, before going over the driver.

"Mr Debono?" I asked.

"Evening. Yes. Mr Foyle is it?"

"That's right. Hello." I got into the passenger seat and we drove off out of Secretary's Lane, round by the Cathedral and into Bomb House Lane. It was a mellow pleasant evening spiced with the excitement and apprehension of the unfamiliar.

"Have you been doing this job long?" I asked for something to say and at the same time ease some of the tension.

"Driving or this one?" asked Mr Debono in reply. "Oh, this one," I explained. "Meeting the Queen's Messenger." Mr Debono squinted one eye as an aid to recollection.

"Must be over two years now, I suppose," he decided. "Not a bad little job. The flights are usually on time, give or take." I nodded in deep comprehension and duly slipped back into awkward silence. We picked up the Glacis Road.

"My first time," I managed to say, stating the obvious in a futile attempt to keep the silence at bay.

"Yes," said the driver, kindly.

"Flight expected in at seven forty-five, isn't it?" I said with another stab at the obvious.

"Huh-huh," was the pleasant retort. We were approaching the aerodrome.

"Barrier is still up," commented Mr Debono, his turn with the obvious. We sped across the runway. We drew up at the chain-link fencing off the landing area.

"*We park here*" was the next contribution to the obvious, adequately complemented by a supportive *I see* from me. Mr Debono settled into a contented rhythm of drumming with fingers on the steering wheel. I occupied myself with guessing the distance I would need to walk into the tarmac when the plane landed. A crackling garble came over the loudspeakers which the experienced Mr Debono deciphered as our flight being announced. A hooting took over as the barrier was lowered.

"You've got plenty of time" said Mr Debono, perhaps noticing my white-knuckle grip on the door handle. "Go over to the duty Inspector inside the fencing and let him know we're here to meet the Queen's Messenger." Time for action. With a *right-o* and a *see you* I was out of the taxi.

I approached the portly figure in khaki shorts standing four-square, hands clasped behind his back, engaged in a lighthouse scan of his surroundings. I found a hollow place somewhere in my stomach. *Inspector Caulfield. Here we go. I knew it. Snag number one. Awkward.* Some months back, on the pretext of swimming in the Bay, Revenue Inspector Caulfield had boarded a 24-foot vessel registered to one Gaston Duval, recently out of Tangiers and Algeciras. Inspector Caulfield was acting on information regarding the owner's smuggling involvement and moving towards impounding the vessel. He was not well pleased when a friend of mine and I rowed up to the vessel with documentary proof that we were the new owners of the vessel. We had secured a bank loan and in a swift transaction bought the Amelie at a knock-down price from Gaston who, aware of his shoulder being about to be tapped by the authorities, repaired in haste to his native Bordeaux.

"Hello Inspector" I said in greeting and was met by a baleful glare.

"What are you doing here? What are you up to?" said Inspector Caulfield narrowing his eyes.

"I'm here to meet the Queen's Messenger," I announced with due propriety.

"Are you indeed? How very nice for you," said the Official testily. "is your little friend about? You haven't bought the plane, have you?" Before I could answer there was a thrilling explosion of power as the plane began to drop. *I must go* I mouthed, pointing to the aircraft which, after a tentative touch-down, screeched towards the end of the runway. I started to walk. The plane made a turning and taxied back into position.

I stood watching the privileged coming down the steps, assessing the likelihood of each conforming to my notion of a Queen's Messenger. There was no mistaking him, the last to appear. He remained at the top of the steps, which I took as my cue to hurry up to him.

"Queen's Messenger, Sir?" I'm from the Secretariat." I held out my red identity card. The supposed QM looked quizzically at the prison photo of the depicted and then at me, before giving a curt nod.

"These the bags, Sir?" I enquired pointing to several deflated canvas bags by his feet and at the same time continuing to state the obvious. Again another nod and I picked up the bags.

"I've got the taxi waiting, Sir." I led the way, processing details of his appearance and manner. *Medium height … stocky … probably ex-military … black long unseasonal coat … battered briefcase … morose … the wan look of one condemned to travel and arrive without joy.*

"Here we are Sir." Another sortie into the obvious, with Mr Debono holding open the back door and giving a civilian quasi-salute.

"Hope you had a pleasant flight, Sir" said Mr Debono with enviable professional ease and being rewarded by a mute compression of the QM's mouth as he got into the taxi.

We passed Inspector Caulfield whom I in turn rewarded with a smug look which said *we have Diplomatic privilege, so sod your Passport Control and baggage search.*

We arrived back at the Secretariat. While Mr Debono attended to the QM, I saw to the padlock and grille, the bags clamped between my knees. Then into the off-duty building, the QM trailing behind me. The cleaners had been and gone, adding the smell of polish and disinfectant to that of the resident nicotine.

We went into Room 9 where the QM sat down with a weary sigh. I remained standing. Presently he appeared to shake himself into purpose and reaching down, hoisted his brief-case on to his lap. He rummaged inside the case, finally settling on several Forms, which he placed side by side on the desk.

"If you would sign these we can get the formalities over," he said without excessive good grace. I examined the lead seals on the bags as required. The canvas bags smelled of old rope. I read the labels attached to the four bags: HE (His Excellency the Governor); CS (Colonial Secretary); FOG (Flag Officer Gibraltar); DSO (Defence Security Officer).

I added impressively ornate flourishes to the Forms laid out on the desk: receipt for the bags; Verification of QM Travel Schedule; Confirmation of QM's expenses. I stored the four bags into the gun-metal storage cabinet and took out another two. It was my turn to request just the one signature as receipt for the two bags labelled CAA (Crown Agents for the Colonies); FO (Foreign Office). These would be collected by the QM in the morning when I would escort him to the airport and see him on his way to wherever his next stop was. I returned the two bags to the cabinet. With judicious help of one knee on the door of the Cabinet with warping inclination, I secured the bags along with the four others for the night.

"Right." The QM rose and we made our way back down to the waiting taxi. "Where am I staying?" asked the QM with the first sign of animation.

"The Rock Hotel, Sir," I was able to inform him. "Mr Debono will pick you up, bring you here and take us to the airport in the morning."

"Right." Mr Debono was waiting with the back door held open. The QM got in.

"See you in the morning," I said to Mr Debono. "And thanks."

"That's alright," he said smiling at the same time raising his eyebrows. "Pick you up at seven."

"Right. I'll be ready." I said. He got into the driver's seat. I tapped on his door in farewell. Then I thought I might have a go at the civilian quasi-salute. Success. The QM gave me a slow nod as the cab started to move.

I yanked the grille shut. Snapped the padlock. The 'pick-up' complete. Tomorrow the 'drop'. I started on my way home. Somewhat stirred and not a little shaken.

Time up

Hear it not ... for it is a knell that summons you to heaven or to hell.

—Shakespeare. *Macbeth.*

How many can claim, hand on heart, to have silenced not one but ten politicians, in quick succession, with them all in full flow. Moreover to have done so by sheer irrefutable, indeed cast-iron, interruption. In a public arena and without infringement of the Law. A humbling experience. On both sides.

* * * * * * * * *

It was a time of posters and promises: of leaflets and loyalties. When worthy citizens of my little town, eminent in their professions or else of independent means, declared themselves as candidates for election to the newly-conceived Legislative Council, where *Honourable* would supplant *Worthy*.

Being myself at the time of civic indifference and of an age without franchise, my favour was not courted and that which might have been of peripheral interest, receded to beyond the horizon: a situation soon to be corrected. With a vengeance.

My well-indulged adolescent paranoia was going at full gallop when I ventured into Mr McCullough's office, in response to his summons.

It was with a perverse sense of vindication, entangled in numb terror, that I received the news that my services in my then present post would no longer be required. Being given to the theatrical, I instantly conjured up a vision of myself in which, barefoot and bedraggled, I dragged myself along cruel streets, with dogs snapping at my heels and arms extended in begging mode. After an interval touching on the infinite, Mr McCullough added that instead I was being temporarily seconded to act as his PA.

Now. Had I not known Mr McCullough to be of Presbyterian persuasion and therefore fully immunised against any form of frivolity, I might have taken the protracted delivery as a joke. Granted a cruel or a simply ill-conceived one, but at least permitting of tearful relief. As it was, desperately as I searched, I failed to detect vestigial amusement in the hatchet features with the punctilious nose, parsimonious lips and accountant eyes peering at me over half-spectacles.

"PA Sir?" I managed to bleat.

"Personal assistant, Foyle. You'll be working with me. I have been designated Returning Officer for the coming elections. I've already squared it with your head of section. Take the rest of the week to tie up loose ends and report to me first thing on Monday."

I left Mr McCullough's office in turmoil, fully convinced that PA was a euphemism for the initial stage of a process prescribed in Civil Service Regulations leading to ultimate dismissal. Although I could string necklaces of faux pas during my probationary period, I wasn't able to alight on any one incident of such serious import as to warrant summary dismissal. I got to thinking that it might rest on inherent character deficiency or perhaps on being of unsuitable background.

In order to sustain myself during the inexorable process which I felt was upon me, I allowed myself the bleak solace that I might have been singled out because being nimble of foot and being well-acquainted with the layout of the building in the course of my suspended duties, I might prove a useful runaround at least.

The rest of the week in the general office was a time of collar-tightening discomfort as I tried to ignore the sullen looks of resentment from my fellows. The senior clerk of the section was particularly affronted and lost no opportunity in expressing the personal inconvenience to himself. With sighs and an air of martyrdom he set about strained telephone calls to various departments in the hope of a replacement, favouring me at regular intervals with baleful looks.

On the Friday, a figure hunched of shoulder and of generally shifty aspect, presented itself at the office. Closer scrutiny confirmed the initial impression with fox-like features and lowered bulging fish-eyes in constant flit. The SC quickly went over to him and engaged him in murmurs, with visual reference from both in my direction.

"Mr Sotto, this is Mr Foyle. He will acquaint you with your duties." Without another word, the SC repaired to his cubicle.

Sotto ... Sotto ... that's right ... yes ... in Medical Administration ... that's right ... on extended probation ... that's right ... something to do with the nursing staff ... yes ... that's right.

I warmed to the downcast Mr Sotto. Here was confirmation of my suspicions: a fellow transgressor crossing my path towards our eventual dismissal.

Finishing time on Friday was a particularly disagreeable occasion with me making a last ditch attempt at protestations of innocence and abhorrence of my new post and only succeeding in piling accusations of hypocrisy on resentment.

And so it was that on the Monday I skulked past my usual place of work towards Mr McCullough's office. A large trestle table had been set up in the office, towards which Mr McCullough beckoned me on entering. He countered my feeble *goodmorning Sir* with an expansive gesture, at odds with his character, over the table, which held an orderly arrangement of files and loose papers together with positioned items of stationery.

"Centre of operation, Foyle," he evinced. "Now, then Foyle. The conduct of the election has to proceed along due protocol. We have to set dates and closing dates. Perceived impartiality is of the essence in what is a great leap forward in democracy."

"Sir."

"Now then. We start with a formal Notice of Proclamation. That to be followed by Submission of Nominations for Canditature etc. etc. With me Foyle?"

"Sir."

"Now then. Here's your first job." He picked up one of the files and took out a sheet. "Now then. Here we are. Take this to Mr Durham, the chap I/C the Typing Pool. We want copies of this addressed to the persons in this list. Starting with H.E. the Governor. A copy for the file of course and a few spares. Tell him to hold on to the stencil just in case. And Foyle."

"Sir."

"Put Mr Durham in the picture vis-à-vis typing for the election. It takes priority. Understand?"

"Sir."

"We shall be working to a tight schedule, Foyle."

"Sir."

"OK. Run along. Come back and we'll go over the timetable and schedule in detail. Off you go."

"Sir."

And so it started and so it went on as far as the paper work was concerned, at any rate. A considerable tax on the Rain Forest. Thankfully, there were also the practicalities, in the pursuit of which I roamed, a deskless nomad, far and wide. Once Mr McCullough's foibles settled into predictability, an exhilarating vista of undreamt-of freedom opened up for me. Of course I needed to keep my eye on the ball *schedule-wise* and fill in any gaps *initiative-wise*.

A widening circle of individuals were roped into the preparations as Polling Day and the Count drew near. As Mr McCollough's front runner, I widened my own circle of resentment from individuals ill-disposed to receiving detailed instructions from a *jumped-up pipsqueak*, even though they were being relayed. A case of *Shoot the Messenger*. I suppose it wasn't so much personal antagonism as a resistance to any change in normal routine, particularly if it was seen to increase the workload. However, these differences had to be worked through. Good humour and common sense usually prevailed. In the odd extreme case of intransigence, there was need to appeal to the individual's sense of self-preservation by reference to his Conditions of Employment as set out in H.M. Civil Service Regulations.

Polling Stations: voting cubicles/tables/chairs/ballot boxes/printed notices (in: out: No Smoking)/ Register of Electors/embossing punch/stapler/Ballot papers/pads/pencils/ruler/rubber bands/sealing wax/ official seal/tapers/matches and the inevitable paper clips.

The Count: extra tables/chairs/PA system and mic./pads/pencils/rubber thimbles/staplers/punch/rubber bands/No Smoking notices/clip-boards/treasury tags/bell and the inevitable paper-clips.

With the benefit of time and distance, I can see that, as I grew in confidence, breezing in and out of the main office to make telephone calls to all and sundry, the sullen glowers of the desk-bound could be justified.

However, relations were to take a turn for the better. With my freedom of movement and malleable schedule, I was able to accommodate daily visits to Galliano's delicatessen during the morning tea break. It occurred to me, being of generous disposition and devious to boot, that I might offer to take orders for sandwiches etc, mentioning that Galliano's had a specialist line in succulent roast pork off the bone on freshly-baked brown bread rolls. I would then sally forth from the Secretariat clutching a substantial list. Henceforth to return and scatter joy among the desk-bound and relief from the powdery digestives.

My popularity was further enhanced when the time came to appoint those employed in the counting of the votes. An internal notice to the effect went out. If I remember rightly, we would be needing six Count Supervisors and some twenty Counting Assistants. Mr McCullough himself contacted the appointed Count Supervisors. These were drawn from heads of sections within the various Departments. When it came to the Counting Assistants Mr M asked me to draw up a list of suitable persons from among my fellows.

Of course, being Government employees there would be no question of payment involved. Instead those chosen would have entitlement to an honorarium: £5.2.6 in the case of the Presiding Officers: £2.12.6 for Counting Assistants. That such figures could be the source of the ripples of excitement and expectation which ran through the building would, in these affluent times, be hard to credit.

Oh, how power corrupts. Could I not have drawn up that list other than by parading, clipboard and pencil in hand, among the desk-bound on repeated occasions, scrutinising my fellows with looks of earnest appraisal?

And oh, the perfidy of the scrutinised with their avowals of camaraderie in return.

* * * * * * * * *

So it was that with a feeling of accomplishment, in restored harmony with my fellows and without undue censure from Mr McCullough, I approached the end of my period as PA.

As it turned out, there was indeed a departure to follow. But before that, on the night of the

Count, an ordeal awaited. One completely unexpected and unforeseen even with the acuity of paranoia. It would involve all ten of the Candidates.

* * * * * * * * * *

It is coming up to seven in the warm mellow evening. Strings of light bulbs wait to come on duty once the sun completes its shift and retires behind the distant hills. The crowd packing the Town Square is in expectant jubilant mood. Occasional chanting lifts in waves followed by bursts of derisive laughter. Faces scan the vaulted open front of the Town Hall, eager for signs of life. At the top of the wide steps leading to the entrance stands a forlorn microphone. A short distance behind it, disconsolate, cruelly exposed to public view, a figure sits at a tiny table.

Me.

Out of sight, in the Green Room, the Candidates strive for composure at the same time in frantic search for the words which strike the right note. Guarding access to the men of the moment, Mr McCullough is under siege from Election Agents, Publicists, hangers-on and the Press. All are avid for details of the proceedings. Mr McCullough holds his ground, his tongue and his hands up in Canute complacency.

I have already been briefed on the details. Earlier on. By Mr McCullough. With finger-wagging emphasis. The Polls close at ten tonight. Then the Count starts. Now each Candidate is being given a two-minute slot for a final pitch at the electorate, with a five-minute interval between each speaker.

Now then, Foyle. Two minutes. Do you understand?

Sir.

Two minutes on the dot. I don't want the hyenas at me.

Hyenas, Sir?

Never mind. You just concentrate on the time. As soon as the speaker utters the first syllable, you hit the stop watch. Then when the hand says two minutes, you clang away like blazes.

Sir.

Now then. Here's the stop-watch. You press and it goes. See? You press again and it stops. Have a little practice on your own. Now then. The Bell. No use getting a silly tinkly little thing. Not with the plebs baying and politicians in full flow. Borrowed this beauty from a naval chap. Solid cast-iron. Mounted on a sensible base. You yank the rope.

Like in boxing matches and firemen Sir?

That's the ticket, Foyle. You just keep clanging.

Sir, do I have to sit right behind the speaker?

Of course you do. You don't want him to be looking at you and getting all nervous in case his time is up. It's what the hyenas said.

Hyenas Sir?

Never mind.

Mr McCullough appears. Walks to the microphone. Ironic applause. He introduces the first speaker and darts off to one side. Out of sight. The man of the moment appears. Mixed reception. The stop-watch feels wet. Mr McCullough fixes on me with wide expectant eyes. The speaker acknowledges the applause with the humble gesture of the undeserving. He pats the air downwards and sallies forth: *fellow citizens* ... I hit the stop-watch and look to Mr M for approval. He nods.

I become eyes. I hear nothing. Feel nothing. I transfer the stop-watch to my left hand. Curl the fingers of my right hand round the bell-rope. Two minutes can be a long time. I tighten the grip on the rope. Ready. I find I lack the nerve to intrude in midsentence. In vain I struggle to find a convenient sentence of neat subject verb object within the convoluted clauses and sub-clauses. I am aware of a sound as of steam escaping from a high-pressure valve. Mr M is hissing at me fit to burst, his arm in violent sideways movement. I yank at the rope, appalled by the incontestable authority of the sound. I have overrun by eighteen seconds.

Forthwith the cronies of nine candidates emerge and set upon Mr M with much pointing at hooked wrists, all united in grievance at the unfair advantage accorded to the ex-speaker. Mr M goes into Gallic shrugs whilst pointing in my direction, effectively diverting a flow of visual venom towards me. I follow suite. Shrug and point lamely at my stop-watch.

The contingent, in complaining mode, begins to make tracks in the direction of the Green Room. Mr M makes time to come over to me so as to enquire about the state of my mental health and express concern about my sleeping pattern. He repairs to the Green Room. I get a few minutes of respite in which to examine my conscience and make reparations towards my conduct with the next turn at the microphone.

The law governing the swing of the pendulum comes into operation and I rob the next speaker of five full seconds. Enough for one affected party to harangue Mr M who disposes of the depleted opposition with a wry twist of the mouth.

On his way to the microphone for the third introduction, Mr M leans over to me and surreptitiously hands me two substantial wads of cotton wool. By way of explanation, I am told they came from the First Aid box and would I plug my ears with them. By way of further explanation I am told that by doing so, I would not be mesmerised by the rhetoric and be fully attendant on the stop-watch. It worked with the remaining speakers and, for me, the evening passed without further incident. During the Count that night and into the early hours for the Declaration I was able to free-pedal, my role virtually at an end.

* * * * * * * * *

I found it difficult to settle back into office routine. In addition to several pressing matters, I had come across the printed letters of one Vincent Van Gogh. I needed to move to the UK and handed in my notice.

On the last day at the office, I walked along the corridors towards the exit in the company of several of my fellows and with that hollow last-time feeling. I had a vague sensation of being insidiously herded, which was confirmed when, on passing by the Boardroom, I received a definite shove through the door.

I found myself in a gathering. There were pickies and bottles of Sherry on the table.

It fell to Mr McCullough to say a few words, appropriate to the pewter-tankard occasion.

He concluded by saying that come the next election, he would be forced to emigrate himself. He said so in a voice and with a look for which I was totally unprepared.

Little Splashes

Jewelled humming bird
Darts sideways into stillness.
Briefly sweetly probes.

*****

Scent of verbena
Conspiring with the night air,
Hinting at secrets.

*****

The unknowable –
Despair in understanding,
Hope in accepting.

*****

Thoughts of past default
Idly stocking the present
With future regret.

Cycle

In the going
Is a coming.
With the terror in the prayer
And the tumult in the resting,
With the clamour in the silence
And the knotting of the entrails,
An inverted resurrection.
In the setting
Is a dawning.
In the ending
A beginning.

Chants

At a time of no tense,
in a crevice on a beach,
crypted of cloud and mountain,
bereft of confluence and the myriad:
a raindrop and a sandgrain.
Constrained in essence,
confounded by substance,
seared by indifference
from the rotated light,
in cold dark stillness
unknowing of the beach.
Innocent of question and self,
lulled in dreams of memory:
chants of deep immensities
heaving in vastness
towards arid undulations
in warm fertile flowing.

The Visit

Fellow Councillors, one and all.
It is with pride and honour
This meeting I now convene,
So to give consideration
To the many vital questions
Attendant on the visit
Of Her Majesty the Queen.

It behoves us, fellow Burghers
To set aside our differences
And bent on common purpose
With diligence and fervour
Our civic duties to discharge.
For glory to Her Majesty
And honour for Her subjects.

I can hardly give expression
To the very humble feeling
And sense of obligation,
That such a signal honour
And uniqueness of occasion
Should fortuitously take place
During our administration.

It falls on us, good Councillors,
As elected representatives
Of a proud and loyal people,
To show our true allegiance.
It is worth that we reflect
That for thrice a hundred years,
We have flown the British flag.

Our frontier we have defended
From foreign land incursion
And repelled attacks from sea
Guarding passage through our Straits.
Our will is further fortified
By undersea resources
And stolid air defences.

Let us then with exultation
Glory in the British Nation.
And with voices raised in prayer
Rally round our Sovereign Monarch.
Almighty God's anointed
Of untainted British blood,
Beacon for our aspirations.

Thereto we now proceed
To focus our attention,
In order of priority
And without discrimination.
The list, we would all agree,
Is headed by our humble
And dutiful presentation.

Imagine, worthy Councillors,
The delight of all our spouses,
As they breathlessly await,
In frocks and hats resplendent,
Their practised curtsies to display.
Our own selves formal of attire
In the dignity of office.

The Royal route has been marked
From Casemates to the Palace.
To proceed along Main Street
And take in the Cathedral.
Our children are to line the route
Waving flags in jubilation,
Their day off school incidental.

Strict attention must be paid
To lines of washing on the route.
No effort must be spared
In sprucing up all frontages,
With due regard for litter,
The overspill from dustbins
And odour from urinals.

Of great concern to all of us
Is the Trocadero Tavern.
With all the raucous singing
And drunken consternation
When the Navy is in town,
Bent on antagonising
Our local population.

Teams of earnest Council workers
Will be deployed the night before.
Some on final sweeping duties,
Some on dowsing of the route.
Others will concern themselves
With securing of the bunting
And the hoisting of the flags.

An imaginative gesture
Has also been put forward.
It is to paint the kerbsides
Along the Royal route
In the colours red white and blue.
A sight most sure to touch
The gracious Sovereign's heart.

There is also the suggestion
That a model true to scale
Of our proud fortifications
Should be carved in local stone
And presented to Her Majesty
As a symbol of esteem
And undying loyal tribute.

And now true and noble Burghers,
I move a period of respite.
That we may return refreshed
To give our consideration,
With all due sensitivity,
To the order of the sitting
At the Ceremonial Banquet.

A point of order if I may,
Most honourable Chairman.
In our keen enthusiasm
For the coming Royal occasion,
We may all have overlooked
That which by unseemly nature
Might the Royal eyes offend.

Councillor, you have the floor,
Please express your grave concern.
It concerns, Honourable Chairman,
The person of Tobailas.
In truth we had forgotten
The existence of the fellow
And his wanderings through our streets.

A sight indeed deplorable.
With open sores and matted hair,
He trudges wild of countenance
As well as with feet bare.
A matter reprehensible
That such a sight be seen,
In civilised society.

We are constrained by Civil Rights,
Inhibiting our actions.
Although, it would be possible,
For a case to be construed
That for the period in question,
The fellow might well benefit
From brief incarceration.

Oops

It is somewhat ironic
That with cataracts excised,
The unfortunate McBride
With a lamppost should collide.

He had walked in admiration
But with lack of registration,
At the blueness of the sky
And the shapes in cloud formation.

Though recovered from concussion,
He retains the complication
Of extreme disorientation
And acute hallucination.

When asked in dutiful concern
Of the wisdom he displayed
When he sought amelioration
In ophthalmic intervention,

Culminating in a venture
With replacement of his dentures
And allied inconveniences,
McBride has ready answer.

A fellow of no mean wit and
Esoteric inclination,
He speaks of double benefit
Of special life enhancement.

For such his new found vision
As to reach beyond the senses,
Giving power of penetration
To the source of revelation.

You Didn't

" … Oh no … she didn't."

"She di-id."

"Dear oh dear."

"Oh yes … and that's not all."

"No?"

"Oh no."

"What?"

"Madam goes on to say I'm a malicious gossip and an evil vindictive bitch … me …"

"No? … er … nooo."

" … That I'm a menace to decent folk and if she had her way she'd have me put down. No wonder my husband died. It was the only way the poor sod could escape. That I'm bitter and twisted and a good job I never had any children. That I'm pure poison. A cancer."

"Nooooo."

"… Oh yes. But don't you worry, I was ready for her … oh yes … I soon settled her hash. I wasn't having any of that … I told her straight … I said to her … I said … *Oh no, I'm not.*"

Onward Christian Soldiers

Not that you might want to. Well, unless you had a certain cast of mind. But if you did, you'd be hard put to see a connection between a particular hymn regularly sung in irreverent fashion, an untoward run on toilet tissue and the appointment of two teachers. You'd need to have inside knowledge to start with. This gathered from day to day observation and from fertile rumours disseminated like the seeds in bird droppings. And then you'd need the distancing of time to give the thread on which to string the scatter of information.

There is comfort, hope and not a little amusement in the thought that whatever the current trends; however numerous the Edicts, Statutes or Acts of Parliament; or well-defined the Aims and Objectives for Education, at the point of delivery there is always the 'undefinable'. The vagaries of the Human Factor. We can take it as read that these exist in abundance with those at the receiving end, but also, in token of a common humanity, with those dispensing it.

Here the focus lingers on the latter with affection and sympathy for they who daily confront the two-sided variables, frequently stretched to reconcile the ideal with the expedient.

On the evidence of that which was to unfold, it could be said that Mr Turnbull the Headteacher might have shown a certain lack of discernment in the appointment of the two individuals concerned. It could be said to be a character trait of Mr Turnbull's, since I myself managed to creep under the net with a total lack of teaching certification and experience. In fairness to the general rigour of the recruiting process, my achievement followed close on two hundred applications across the Realm, the majority of which were not acknowledged let alone considered. Still, my desperation was rewarded at the eleventh hour with the post of Assistant Art Teacher in a Secondary Modern School for Boys in Middle Earth. On the other hand, Mr Turnbull might have been in full possession of all his faculties and simply 'cutting according to the cloth', seeing that I, along with my fellow appointees were the only applicants for the respective posts.

Personal merit apart, we of the staff rejoiced in the appointments bringing as they did two extra pairs of hands to man the pumps and help keep the ship at navigable level above the waterline. Of more immediate import came the relief from not being obliged to continue caulking the gaps in the timetable by taking extra classes in foreign subjects.

Mr Tredwell joined us well into the Autumn Term with Mr Fanshawe following some ten days later. Both came, as they say, out of the blue to where presumably they returned. Quite promptly, as things turned out.

As Assistant Music Teacher, Mr Tredwell took over a non-existent Music Department resourced with three recorders, a tambourine and five music stands. The school piano languished under cover and padlock in the Assembly Hall. He was, at least, allocated full use of a classroom. Unlike me, for although appointed as Assistant Art Teacher in a non-existent Department equipped with one ream of newsprint, twelve HB pencils and a pack of terracotta, I found myself cutting my pedagogical teeth with a spell in an end corridor as the result of a double booking.

From the start Mr Tredwell displayed a reticence and inclination to the reclusive beyond that expected of one in unfamiliar surroundings. It will be appreciated that such traits are not ideally suited to a milieu peopled by twenty staff and over four hundred other beings. He was however assiduous in their pursuit, never to my knowledge venturing into the staffroom or dining room, preferring to take his Ryvita, cheese and apple in his foundling conservatoire. The prospect of his subsequently enforced debut in that signal school morning assembly must have registered significantly on the Daunting Scale. Although one cannot say with certainty that it was the sole cause of Mr Tredwell's departure, it may well have precipitated it. Again none of us were aware of Mr Turnbull's aversion to that particular hymn or of his insistence that Mr Tredwell performed at that assembly. Mr Tredwell had requested permission to be excused from assemblies on religious grounds. The perceived wisdom in the staffroom viewed the request as symptomatic of sub-clinical agoraphobia.

If approached by a colleague in an open space, perhaps on school business, Mr Tredwell adopted an abrupt pleasantness of manner. With head inclined attentively while wringing his hands and looking intently at his accoster's face, he silently mouthed the words being addressed to him. A most disconcerting experience for which I can personally vouch. On one occasion when we made our way to our respective classes in the top corridor, I made bold to enquire as to how he was settling in. Mesmerised by seeing my words mouthed back at me, I found myself answering 'very well thank you' to my own question.

Mr Fanshawe's brief was to fill the spiritual vacuum, coming as Assistant Religious Education Teacher in a non-existent R.E. Department deploying Gideon Bibles without number, several slim books on the life of Jesus illustrated in watercolour and a poster enumerating the Seven Deadly Sins with graphic depiction of attendant repercussions.

Whereas Mr Tredwell could have been said to be in the vigour of his middle years, Mr Fanshawe had turned a downward corner. He presented an air of grey serenity and studied courtesy. An effect enhanced by venerable grey of hair and demob suit of the same colour with extravagant lapels and over-emphatic turn-ups. A tiny gold cross self-effacingly sanctified the left lapel, with more clarion adornment of the right with a substantial green locomotive banded with red proclaiming membership of a railway enthusiasts' group. At some indeterminate level, I found the relative weights, if not the combination, unsettling. A clash of symbols, one might say.

A model of sobriety, Mr Fanshawe moved among us with other-worldly detachment, his countenance fixed in that humourless pouting set of the upper lip often found in persons of entrenched piety. He saw himself as a force for good and, redolent of good intentions, came well disposed to lay down his quota of pavings along that road which is said to lead to the Nether Regions.

School life buzzed along, the days divided by insistent bells signalling change of lessons, respite for exercise, feeding time and final release. Within it, the new appointees swirled to confront their personal clashes with base realities.

Mr Fanshawe increasingly displayed the wan wide-eyed look of the traveller who, setting out joyfully towards the City of Golden Spires, finds his progress blocked by a sheer escarpment calling for the use of pitons and crampons.

The details of Mr Tredwell's sojourn remained largely undisclosed owing to the rare sightings of the traveller himself, with any indications reliant on the intercepted whisperings of the alumni. His area of timetabled activity was confined to First and Second Years, leaving the Music Teacher available for the more pressing duty of substitution for colleagues in respect of illness, dental appointments, study courses, relatives' funerals and Wimbledon.

Of a puzzling nature was the rumour that those pupils instructed in Music were expected to attend lessons in possession of a comb. The conjecture that Mr Tredwell might be prompted by a concern with coiffure was difficult to reconcile with the teacher's personal appearance, which vacillated between unkempt and undecided. The unusual requirement might have sat more comfortably if originating from Mr Fanshawe, from whence there might be the connection with pride in personal appearance as respect for the *Temple of God*.

As regard the question of the combs, I found myself in a position able to contribute to staffroom musings. During one spell of playground duty, my attention was drawn to a gathering of inmates in a suspicious huddle. Using available cover and stealth, I was able to pounce on the gathered, assuming nefarious activity. These turned out to be First and Second Years. Combs of varying sizes and colours were being examined and compared with general merriment.

As practitioners in the peripheral subjects of Music, R.E. and Art, Messrs Tredwell, Fanshawe and myself occupied the distancing wastes of the top corridor. Often during those days following their appointments, there was evidence of untoward classroom behaviour in particular when Mr Fanshawe's classes comprised the disaffected Fourth Year Leavers. The disruption at times reached Biblical character with Mr Fanshawe's entreaties a lone voice 'Crying in the wilderness'. Short of the situation becoming extreme or assistance being sought, it was prudent not to intervene and quell youthful exuberance, since in the long run it would further undermine Mr Fanshawe's authority, if only in his own eyes.

The goings-on in Mr Tredwell's classes, in keeping with his own disposition, were altogether of a less determinate nature. I had for some time been aware of a *vhoosing* sound along the corridor, which I put down to up-draught coming from the well of the stairway opposite my classroom. Leaving the asylum in the charge of the inmates, I went out into the corridor and secured the fire-doors, but the sound persisted.

Following the audio trail, I ended up outside the door to Mr Tredwell's classroom. Ear to door the *vhoosing* sound took on another character. It rose and fell between an agonising moan and a breathy hysterical wail. The sound did not appear to emanate from one single larynx venting distress for it rose and fell in concert and to a pattern of sorts. I concluded that Mr Tredwell might be tracing the ethnicity of music and regaling the class with recorded Aboriginal examples.

Then there was that staff meeting. Nothing to do with classroom behaviour. Or so we might have thought then. We had to wait for that assembly on the last week of term to put two and two together. Anyway, we are sitting there. In comes Mr Turnbull and starts handing out the agenda on skimpy bits of paper. Item one: Toilet paper. Mr Turnbull sits down and makes a big thing of coughing and clearing his throat. All the staff have got this blank expression. When Mr Turnbull gets going, it seems he's been *approached by Mr Hoffnung regarding the exceptional run on paper in the male staff toilet.* But we know different. We know Mr Hoffnung the Caretaker. By temperament and office, tyrant of All He Surveys. We know it would be more on the lines of *look here Headmaster, I've got more important duties than running after a bunch of teachers, seeing they haven't run out of Bronco every five minutes.* Then Mr Turnbull's diplomacy goes into sledgehammer mode with the information that he's had a word with the *in-house catering* and apparently by the vehemence of the retort, Mr Turnbull had been obliged to consider other sources to account for Mr Hoffnung's concern. He settled for a virulent gastric bug, an explanation which might mollify Mr Hoffnung. But which apparently didn't. For even allowing for the editing in the retelling, Mr Hoffnung had expressed thoughts on the teaching profession, while disparaging Mr Turnbull's explanation of possible cause by pointing out that no similar profligate use of tissue was evident in the Boys' toilets. Further, the extravagant use in the Staff toilets was not confined to individual sheets of Bronco but to whole boxes, complete with cardboard packaging.

I wouldn't go as far as to think that Mr Turnbull consciously appointed Messrs Tredwell and Fanshawe, mid-term as he did with other existing subject vacancies unfilled, because of school assemblies, the Monday one to be precise and his aversion to that hymn. We sometimes do things from deeper levels and justify them to ourselves with rational motives.

He was, of course, within his rights to insist that Mr Tredwell should participate in assemblies. There was a piano in the hall after all and Music was his thing. Well, in the end Mr Tredwell relented and made his debut at the last assembly of term, which no doubt in Mr Turnbull's eyes was not a felicitous occasion, although the same might not be said of the rest of the school.

There was no such complication in Mr Fanshawe taking over the spiritual direction of Corporate Worship. However, the substance and tedium of his deliveries may have forced Mr Turnbull's hand in wanting to liven the miasma with piano accompaniment of the singing at least.

Inter-departmental liaison hadn't been invented at the time and consequently Messrs Tredwell and Fanshawe prepared for that assembly in isolation other than with instruction from Mr Turnbull that the hymn appropriate to disband his charges should be 'Onward Christian Soldiers'.

Mr Turnbull himself espoused, if not a muscular, certainly an assertive Christianity. He had risen from a background of Sunday School complemented by the Scout Movement and voluntary work with St John's Ambulance. He presented as an advocate of the *mens sano in corpore sano* school of thought. Not withstanding a hacking smokers' cough which conveniently alerted everyone within a radius of some sixty yards of his presence when on the prowl.

Of course, we had no inkling of how that hymn must have affected him week in week out. It seems curious that it had to be that hymn in every Monday morning assembly. Why not ring the changes. Perhaps Mr Turnbull didn't want to draw attention to his discomfiture or perhaps he felt there to be Christian mileage in enduring. We'd have been none the wiser but for his retirement speech in the staffroom. Perhaps, contrary to his nature, the occasion called for a humorous quip. He said that, of course, he would miss working in our midst, but most of all, praise the Lord, he would not have to start the week listening to that wretched hymn.

The opening line to the offending hymn ran: 'Our souls we raise to the Lord'. A noble sentiment and appropriately Christian aspiration with which to start the working week. However, by a mixture of poor enunciation and covert gleeful subversion from the assembled, it emerged as: 'Arseholes we raise to the Lord'.

When I started in my appointment, morning assemblies had a rough and tumble quality which on first encounter had me wishing I had listened to my father and gone into a trade.

Pupils converged on the Entrance Hall from four directions and poured into the venue for worship with a boisterous bonhomie, as if entering a football stadium. A first come first served situation ensued with favoured seats being taken and others reserved for close acquaintances. Mr Altringham the Deputy Head, standing on the raised apron of the stage with hands joined in front and the impassive countenance of a Red Indian Chief, bore silent witness to the influx.

As the hall filled with the arrival of classes, the ambience lifted with animated exchanges across rows and aisles. When the flow stemmed Mr Altringham went from 'stand easy' to 'attention'. *Quiet*. Repeated thrice in crescendo from hopeful to bellow. *Stand*. More opportunities for scraping of chair and discreet shoving. *Quiet*.

Then Mr Turnbull entered, Bible held forward with arm angled in Sergeant-major fashion when holding his stick. As likely as not Mr Turnbull might interrupt his progress along the right aisle to berate some individual vis-à-vis his appearance or deportment. Ascending three steps, the Head approached the lectern stage centre. With great deliberation, while scanning the assembled, the Bible would be placed on the lectern and opened at the red tape marker.

Mr Turnbull announced the hymn for the day, followed by extravagant throat clearing to offset the coming of a coughing fit. Then the singing. A cappella. A ragged affair with only the voices of Messrs Turnbull and Altringham discernible amid the drone. *Sit*. With an irritable gesture from the Head. *Quiet*. From the Deputy. The Bible opened at the green marker for the homily. Mr Turnbull read the passages in a level tone without inflection, conserving his energy after the singing. The Bible closed emphatically. An unnerving pause and then the launch of a tirade in acerbic tone in which some aspect of current pupil behaviour fell short of the virtues embodied in the homily.

In the cowed silence the Head nodded to Mr Altringham, at the same time reaching for something from the small drop-leaf table behind him. *Aldwinckle … Bunton … Cullings … Dalrymple … Ennis … Fortescue etc.* The named by the Deputy detached themselves from their fellows and lined up in the order called at the bottom of the three steps. *Aldwinckle … one.* The renamed mounted the steps in the manner of one about to receive some commendation. At the lectern, he held out one hand. *Whoosh.* The Headmaster's cane descended. Exit Aldwinckle. *Bunton … two. Cullings … one. Dalrymple … three. etc.* The going rate was: one for missing the previous day's after-school detention; two hits for two misses; three for persistent misconduct. Having rendered unto God, the assembled were dismissed to render unto Caesar.

Life then was lived according to the time. The time before the coming of the Comprehensive system; before the number in the school trebled; before it became mixed; before laying a hand on a child's shoulder could be construed as assault or molestation.

We knew every child's first name, although familiarity was not encouraged. There was a rough and tumble, often humorous, tenor to daily life, as was to be expected with over four hundred boys corralled in the unnatural setting of a school. In addition, as a consequence of the Eleven Plus, there existed to varying degrees in the eyes of the pupils, implied failure in being relegated to the Secondary Mod. It was part of our job to dispel such perception by demonstrating that types of abilities vary as much as the outlets for them.

The cane was simply a fact of life. The majority of the instructed managed without any contact with it during the period of their internment. In some circles it was regarded as a desirable Rite of Passage. The prerogative for chastisement rested principally with the Headteacher, although on occasions other senior staff might have recourse to it. In all instances a full record, including tariff, was kept in the Punishment Book.

Personally I never used the bamboo, being of the belief that a quick light cuff, before things got out of hand, was less damaging than the cold disdain in institutional punishment. The approach presupposes an equal willingness to ruffle hair or pat shoulder when the occasion merited it. Further, it presupposes that there are parameters in place for acceptable behaviour, applicable on both sides, which are seen to be fair and not dependant on mood and which require the recognition that with the unequal advantage in numbers, the adults' tolerance should not be tested to the limits.

Like most situations, even that appertaining to the administering of corporal punishment, life can have its lighter side. Of course, it much depends on what side of the fence you find yourself at any given time. The case of Lanky McKenzie, a serial offender, comes to mind.

During one auspicious assembly, Lanky took his regular place at the foot of the three steps. On cue at '*McKenzie … three*', Lanky ascended on stage and took his position by the lectern. It then appeared that he experienced a severe attack of stage fright for, with an expletive relevant to the occasion, he bounded down from the stage and proceeded along the centre aisle with velocity.

Displaying great presence of mind, Mr Turnbull acted. He passed the cane to Mr Altringham as might a relay runner pass a baton, at the same time giving a silent hand signal to the Deputy in the manner of a Shepherd to a collie in pursuance of the retrieval of an errant sheep to the flock.

Having to descend the stage in decorous manner via the steps, Mr Altringham put himself at a disadvantage in the chase. However, such was his zeal that, to the appreciation of the assembled, he significantly reduced the discrepancy distance-wise. He, nonetheless, much to the general dismay, suffered a setback in the interests of personal safety. He was obliged to come to an abrupt halt as Lanky dashing through the glass double doors, had the forethought to swing them back violently. At the third swing, Mr Altringham resumed the chase. As the distance of the action from the hall increased, the assembled strained to listen in a charged silence which left the Head at a loss. There was a wave of palpable relief as the action appeared to draw closer again. There were further expletives from Lanky of a personal nature with placatory sounds from Mr Altringham. Then the sound of steps on stone, followed by thumping on the ceiling of the hall, indicating that the action had moved up the main staircase onto the first floor.

Unwisely Mr Turnbull dismissed the assembly, whereupon the whole school had their classes on the top floor. Lanky had gone to ground in the library. Mr Altringham stood panting outside the closed door gathering resolve. It may be that Lanky found Mrs Baltimore the librarian more of a threat than Mr Altringham. He dashed out of the library into the arms of his pursuer and a grapple promptly ensued.

McKenzie was grimly silent, his concentration on swaying and dancing in avoidance mode. Mr Altringham, denied the convenience of a proffered hand in acquiescence, was intent on exacting justice on Lanky's lower extremity. With an admirable feinting action, much appreciated by the packed staircase and top corridor, Mr Altringham wrong-footed McKenzie and was able to discharge his duty.

The moment had passed. McKenzie ceased the struggle and appeared to come to his senses. Mr Altringham seemed to notice the bystanders and demanded to know in a wheezing voice whether *anybody have classes to go to*. In the dispersal, Mr Altringham's similar enquiry of the subdued Lanky was met with *Geography, Sir*. Followed by *you better get there quickly then*.

The interminable Autumn Term dragged to a close. With the end in sight, the expectation brought a levity of spirit and some distraction from hostilities. The last day in particular was a testing time. The subject timetable was abandoned and pupils confined to Form Rooms. It was then the task of the Form Teacher to provide the in-house entertainment on the countdown to the bell for early dismissal. That last day's morning school assembly was to add another element to the usual high frequency expectancy.

Over the weeks, Mr Fanshawe's conduct of corporate worship, as indeed his manner, had somewhat hardened. His previously embracing disposition registering a permanent look of distaste. The standard homily, derived from lengthy tracts in the Old Testament, increasingly inclining towards Divine Justice rather than Mercy. It may be that if not Mr Fanshawe himself, then Mr Turnbull would have welcomed Mr Tredwell's impending contribution, hopefully bringing respite with the power of music to enchant.

It may also have been the case that given time and adequate Capitation Allowance, Mr Tredwell might have taken school music to symphonic level, on the surmise that from little acorns mighty oaks can grow. Of course the conjecture remained academic. As things stood, Mr Tredwell had shown the same reluctance in going anywhere near the Hall piano as he had in venturing inside the staffroom. His area of activity within his subject, given his natural reticence and his confinement to the wastes of the top corridor, was a closed book.

Of course, so and so should have said this or some other so and so should have done that. When things take on an unexpected turn for the worse, it's all too easy to think that. But certainly it wouldn't have been too much to expect that the R.E. teacher might at some point mention the coming assembly to the Music teacher, if only to agree on the order of the service. Similarly Mr Turnbull's involvement might have gone some way beyond telling the reluctant Mr Tredwell that the hymn 'Onward Christian Soldiers' was an appropriate one on which to disband for the holiday. We sin by omission just as effectively as by commission.

Whatever the shortcomings of Mr Tredwell's contribution as musical director in his inaugural appearance in corporate worship, at least it resolved several unanswered questions. Among them was that which concerned Mr Hoffnung regarding the Bronco. It is doubtful whether the information was ever relayed to the caretaker. If it had, Mr Tredwell would have been spared a dressing-down by the zealous official. For Mr Tredwell failed to materialize after the recess. As did Mr Fanshawe.

Mr Turnbull, who had delegated the conduct of the service, had been obliged to resume control in the interests of discipline. He resolved the situation by abruptly ending what had been intended as an extended occasion, by dismissing the assembled to the care of their respective Form Teachers to await the final bell.

The proceedings got off to a shaky start in that Mr Fanshawe, in announcing the hymn for the occasion, had assumed Mr Tredwell to be waiting to make his entrance to the stage from the wings. In the awkward silence which followed, all heads turned towards a grating sound coming from the back of the Hall. Mr Tredwell stood holding open the double doors perhaps either reluctant to enter or in some confusion as to whether he had arrived at the right venue.

An impatient beckoning gesture from Mr Fanshawe might have reassured him on either count, since he proceeded along the centre aisle with a loping stride. He was followed by some twenty cowed First Years bunched together, who increasingly withdrew within themselves at the mounting murmurs and random taunts by the assembled *in soto voce*.

Arriving at the front of the Hall, there was some confusion among the arrivals in deciding whether they were expected to ascend on to the stage or face the assembled at ground level. Mr Fanshawe cast an agonised glance in the direction of the seated Head, who parried with a grim countenance. With an executive decision, Mr Fanshawe gave another impatient gesture towards the stage, hurriedly removing the lectern to a place of safety.

Finally the youngsters were in position, arrayed in a single file facing the auditorium. Mr Tredwell with his back to it, perilously close to the edge of the apron.

Mr Fanshawe, lecternless, once more announced the hymn of the day, looking pointedly at the music provider. Mr Tredwell muttered something at the First Years. He did so several times, moving along the line facing him to make sure that those at the extremities heard his hoarse laboured instruction. There followed a general fumbling as the instructed extricated combs of varying size and colour from disparate pockets. The revelation evinced barely suppressed hilarity from the body of the Hall. The musicians got ready their instruments using sheets of tissue paper and gazed nervously at the Conductor.

Mr Tredwell raised both arms. He lowered them in a flying movement. Sporadic drone started from the auditorium as the assembled made ragged engagement with the opening line of 'Onward Christian Solders'. The musicians blew: *Vvov Vvov Vviv Vvav Vvor – Vvov/Vvav.*

Editor's note: The arrangement of a comb and tissue paper is called a Kazoo. The Concise Oxford Dictionary defines it thus: *a toy musical instrument into which player sings or hums.*

2012: A Sock Oddity

Before my wife and I, in our different ways, took God to task regarding His existence, we were practising Catholics although, for my part, I never did attain any standard to speak of.

Once, as a rebuff to hard times, we treated ourselves to a day-trip to London and looked around the Ideal Home Exhibition in Earl's Court. There, perhaps as an aid to our wishes, we splashed out on an expensive Family Bible: a splendid tome bound in ivory calf leather with gilt-edged pages, excellent reproductions of Old Masters' paintings pertinent to the text and an enticing section in vellum for the entries of special family occasions. Over the years, we have kept the entries up-to-date, with the joyful ones far outweighing the sad ones.

The Bible became a sort of convenient repository for certificates and the like, mainly to do with the children as they grew up. Among the little treasures contained between the printed pages are two handwritten ones in pencil by Jonathan, our first-born, when he was six years old. They are a touching and poignant reminder of Jon's gentle nature, made precious with his untimely death.

Nonetheless, also true to his nature, the pages are not without a certain quirky humour. They contain one particular line which must seem curious coming from a little boy. It can be put down to Jon's sensitivity or else to the importance of that which he refers to within the day-to-day life of the family. Jon's pages are here shown in facsimile together with transcripts to help with the sometimes creative spelling.

* * * * * * * * *

Life does have its mysteries: from the Bermuda Triangle to the persistence of teaspoons in the bowl after the washing-up. In similar vein, there is the mystery behind the disappearance of odd socks with the consequent accumulation of their bereft partners. It was a mystery of ongoing concern when our six daughters were of school age and white socks were obligatory as part of the school uniform.

Those reared in innocence might surmise that white socks are white socks are white socks. Not so. There are, of course, obvious differences of size and length. But when it comes to pairing them, we enter the Twilight Zone. To achieve a matching pair is to contend with the odds set against it. You tend to have to operate on a system of elimination rather than selection.

You may start off with two socks selected for their whiteness. For let it be known that whiteness is relative to the number of washes a sock has undergone. Then length needs to be ascertained by stretching the articles, since they are likely to have emerged from the tumble-dryer hunched up in disorientation. The next hurdle is thickness of material. This can vary between fluffy towelling, stringy cotton and numerous mixtures. Are the two candidates for selection plain, patterned or textured? Here we enter the minefield. If plain, do they have loose or elasticated tops? If textured, is it overall or running vertically in ribbing in bands? If so, are the gaps between the bands plain? If patterned, again is it overall or sectioned? Are the patterns based on diamonds, herring-bone, floral, radial themes or piercing? From time

Facsimile of unsolicited 'testimonials' from Jonathan, age six.

Daddy

You are wonderful
You are nice
You are beautiful

You look after us
You earn money
You share things
You are a nice man.
You got us a nice house
You do lovely pictures for us
You fetch us drawing paper
You fetch mummy's shopping
You bought me a bed
You go to school and work
You married a wonderful wife
You buy my clothes
You buy my shoes
You play football with me
You give me money sometimes
You give mummy presents and things
You do everything you can for us.

Mummy

You are a beautiful mummy
You are a nice mummy
You are a wonderful mummy

You do the washing up
You do the dinner
You do the beds
You do the nappies
You do the tea
You do the cleaning
You do the breakfast
You do the bathing
You do the radishes
You do the letters
You do the buying
You do the money for dinners
...... You do the pairing socks ......
You do the winning
You do the surprises
You do the baking
You do everything

Transcript of 'testimonials'.

to time, the prospective wearers would point out discrepancies in the pairings which were quite beyond the discriminative powers of the in-house pairer.

The Sunday evening ritual entailed shoes being polished and fresh uniforms arrayed on hangers in readiness for the Monday morning scramble. A set straight-forward routine. Until it came to pairing six sets of white socks. Out would come the bloated odd-socks bag from its hook in the closet. With the combined resources of the bag, the newly-laundered socks and due diligence, some pairings might be achieved but always with further additions to the distended bag.

Once, out of perverse interest, a count of the contents of the odds bag yielded ninety-nine odd socks.

We sought commiseration with other households only to discover that although the phenomenon of the disappearing odd socks was not unknown, our own household was a *hot-spot* for manifestations.

One family volunteered a solution to the problem of perpetual pairing. It was a practice which they had themselves instigated with surgical effectiveness. The family comprised Dad, Mum, a boy and girl. The solution was the issue of Marks and Spencers plain black socks of one size for all. The bench mark for the size was determined by Dad, a man of impressive build. The rest of the family had the option of folded socks underfoot or sock heels half way up the calf. The same principle, though exacting less personal toll, was adopted for towels, bed sheets and pillow cases.

We ourselves periodically cut our losses, emptying the odds bag and restocking over the Summer holidays, turning over the bag to fallow before replanting in the September.

In the fullness of time, the once-white-socks wearers flew the nest and the phenomenon abated. Now all mothers, some grandmothers, perhaps they perpetuate the mystery or encounter other phenomena enshrined in family life.

However, what we imagined to be a cure to the problem, turned to be a period of respite. For, here we are in 2012 and the mystery has once again surfaced. True, with just the two of us, we have no need for an odd-sock bag and can manage adequately with just a small bedside odd-sock drawer.

We have puzzled long, assiduously re-living the journey of the laundry from the corner basket in the bathroom to the washing machine in the kitchen, to the tumble dryer in the garage. We have scrutinised the basket and revolved by hand the empty drums of the two machines. In unguarded moments, we have cross-examined each other regarding standards of personal hygiene and practice. All to no avail: without even the comfort of being able to blame the girls.

We have always kept dogs of medium to large size. When Cassie our last one died, we did the sensible thing to accord with our ages and recently downsized house. We got a small pup. Cleo is a Jack Russell Shitsu cross. She is very vocal and most determinedly affectionate. She understands what we tell her and leaves us in no doubt about what she wants to tell us. We reached a point when we felt that she was becoming too 'humanised' and would benefit from the company of another dog.

By chance a friend who breeds and shows dogs, mentioned a pup from a recent litter which, not conforming to breed standards for showing, was available as a pet ... and were we interested. The *Ah* factor kicked in.

The pup arrived. A Japanese Chin. After three years, we are still reluctant to describe it as a dog in the general sense. He runs like a rabbit, climbs like a monkey, has the fastidiousness of a cat, doesn't bark, doesn't wag his tail, spins round when excited. Although a fine specimen, he was short of Kennel Club standard for the breed by having one undescended testicle. We got him at half price. Paying by the testicle, so to speak.

I was all for naming him 'Adolf' after an individual similarly challenged. To underpin my choice, I made him a lovely little armband, red with a white circle bearing a swastika, and paraded him before the family. For some reason, this appeared to freak them out and he was name Louis.

In addition to the peculiarities aforementioned Louis displays other traits which don't go by the manual. Although he doesn't bark as such, he can summon up a terse commanding sound, which he uses at times with uncanny precision by the clock. He does so a) when it's time for us to get up in the morning, b) when it's time for his morning and evening walks, c) when it's time for his feed, d) when it's time for us to come down from our studies for the evening, e) when it's time for him to go upstairs for his biscuit before settling down for the night.

His most puzzling trait has to be his obsessive practice of Feng Shui, which presumably can be attributed to his Japanese connection. On a daily basis, the bedding from his box; cushions from sofa and armchairs; as well as any cloths or clothing within reach are, with great determination, dislodged on to the floor. There they are arranged with fastidious precision to his satisfaction. Only then will he select one item on which to curl up with a contented sigh.

I was crawling under my wife's desk to re-connect a computer terminal into the multi-socket.

There.

An arrangement in grey, fawn and black socks.

His Louisship luxuriating in contentment, slender front paws elegantly crossed.

The mystery of the 2012 Sock Oddity: solved.

The culprit.

Where Have All the Cavors Gone

"Refrigeration?" I queried, off-beam as usual with my defective hearing.

"Refiguration," repeated George Lustre in a tone terse and at the same time apologetic. Then it went quiet and I thought I'd lost him.

"Listen," he said, coming on again. "I can't talk over the phone. Is there any chance you could come over? I wouldn't ask if it wasn't important. Only … well… you see … it wouldn't be any use me going to you."

"I daresay I could manage it. My time is pretty much my own these days." Intrigued as I was, I kept my voice level.

"Marvellous," said George Lustre in soft falsetto, as if to himself. "The only thing is" he continued, his voice taking on an anxious edge, "it would have to be at least two days before the seventeenth of this month. "You see, I fly to Estonia on that date."

"It shouldn't be a problem," I reassured him.

"You'd be doing me … not just me … a great favour." George Lustre's voice lightened into gratitude.

"Leave it with me," I said. "I'll check train times and get back to you.

I had good reason to be intrigued. I will also admit to being flattered. That phone conversation was my first and only contact with George Lustre for the best part of thirty years. I recognised him, with a start, on the TV programme 'The Sky at Night'. I got in touch with the BBC and embarked on a trail of enquiries and guarded answers which eventually yielded George Lustre's contact number. On a whim I rang him. After all, it's not every day that you finally decide to buy a microscope.

* * * * * * * * *

George Lustre ('Pearly' to some: 'Lack-Lustre' to others) and I became close for a time while studying for our 'A' Levels. It could be said that it was more of an alliance than a friendship: one formed by two individuals walking away backwards from the complexities of life and bumping into each other. Granted, our retreats were differently motivated but they did converge on spurious common ground.

We had both attended the same prestigious Grammar School where social differences were assessed and managed by ambitious parents, in Lustre's case effectively vetoing association with a scholarship boy whose parentage, in turn, viewed education with suspicion, seeing it as an ill-fated attempt to rise above one's station. The more disparate intake of the Sixth Form College, together with sexual preoccupation and the need to rebel, made it possible if not mandatory, for gender and class barricades to be breached. Thus, unlikely associations were spawned, which in the main, carried little hope of surviving away from the College's rarefied air. So it was with George Lustre and myself.

The first acknowledgement of each other's existence took place amid the hullabaloo of the students' Cafeteria during break one morning. Waiting in queue to be served, we exchanged awkward grimaces. To these were added diffident nods on a subsequent occasion. The breakthrough came during yet another occasion when, reluctant to join in the hilarity of the over-subscribed tables, we hovered around the area between the vending machines and the toilets. Our attention was largely focussed on avoiding first degree burns to fingers as we sought to maintain grip on the token rim of the extremely thin and flexible white plastic cups purporting to contain black coffee. It may have been as a distraction from pain that I ventured forth with the abrupt inappropriateness of the socially inept.

"I've been reading H.G. Wells," I postulated and took an inordinate gulp of liquid, thereby transferring my concern with fingers to an internal furnace. If Lustre was aware of my discomfiture he showed no sign of it. Instead, he took a measured sip with a prissy little intake of breath.

"Interesting hypotheses," countered G.L. at length as if thinking aloud and we both relapsed effortlessly into normal disconnection.

The following day we gathered sufficient resolve to occupy a vacant table where, able to rest the cups thereby neutralizing their threat, we toddled further towards familiarity. After that, we made bold to widen the field of operation to include the Common Room and in due course, our respective quarters.

We did share an interest of sorts in Science Fiction. Notably in the writings of H.G. Wells, C.S. Lewis and latterly Arthur C. Clarke. However, to claim that it was that interest which bound us together, would be on a par to making that claim in respect of a common interest in breathing. For our association, while it lasted, had something of the passivity and reflex nature of that function. An interest of convenience rather than of passion, so to speak: a semblance of social interaction for two otherwise displaced individuals.

From the viewpoint of armchair psychology, Lustre fronted a remote phlegmatic disposition in contrast to my mercurial flitting about. As I got to know him, I discovered that he burned with a heat no less intense for the absence of flame. His focus on his studies was total, fixed with unblinking reptilian stare on Physics and Mathematics. Not overly liked, he was nonetheless respected, not least by his tutors. These, although frequently embarrassed by being found wanting in the intensity of Lustre's light, bore him little resentment. For Lustre had a disarming innocence about him and his instructors found comfort in the knowledge that brilliance is at times visited on near-imbeciles.

The Science Fiction connection did not make for cosy chats between two chaps indulging a shared enthusiasm. It was more on the lines of abrupt utterances: as of a recalcitrant motor cycle kick-started, spluttering to silence and being restarted. I lapped up the 'Fiction', agog at Wells' Selenites, Eloi, Morlocks and Martians; Lewis' hrossa, Sorn, pfifltriggi, Oyarsa and Eldila as well as Clarke's less determinate Higher Intelligences. For his part, Lustre scrutinised the 'Science'. He made what I thought were puzzling observations on *alternative systems of propulsion, undiscovered highways* and *space within matter*. He did so using mathematical argument which made my neural pathways, accustomed to dealing with the warm flux of fantasy, go cold. I daresay the reverse might have applied to him in regard to myself but for different reasons.

Our interaction upgraded to quite a different footing after I bought the cine camera. During one of my unaccountable flittings, I had found myself in London and inside the Aladdin's Cave that went by the name of Brunnings in Holborn. There I saw and was captivated by a lovely little black Bolex cine camera with cute turretted lenses and lustrous goose-pimpled black leather body enhanced with chrome trim. At the time, the new Super 8 format was laying siege to the old Standard 8, so the little wind-up Bolex came at greatly reduced price.

I showed off my prize to Lustre in the hope of it extending the scope of our chats and was promptly regaled with a lecture on the Principles of the Persistence of Vision whereby the single frames on film achieved continuous motion. Chastened but undaunted, I repaired to my quarters to ponder on the use to which I might put my little treasure other than pointing it at all and sundry with the risk of incurring wrath. That night I tossed and turned in supplication to the Muse. It was in the early hours when she relented and I was visited by a double epiphany in the form of the painfully obvious. *What does one do with a cine camera?* Make films. *What kind of films?* Science Fiction films, what else. Here was the justification for my unlikely association with Lustre. Together we would produce a Science Fiction film. I could let rip with the fiction: he would legitimise the science. Simple.

I gushed out the idea to Lustre at our next get-together, having already hatched a storyline for the film. In summary it stretched originality, involving a visitation by a well-disposed Alien with attendant repercussions. Lustre listened abstractly, his mouth tightening.

"And how do you propose that this … well-disposed Alien … travels to Earth?" he posed, at the same time inclining his head sideways and reshaping his mouth in a pitying smile.

"Da-raaah," I crowed in triumph, extravagantly displaying what had bulged in my trouser pocket: a geode roughly the size and shape of an avocado.

"You see?" I explained. "He travels inside this. Not fully formed. Like in a fertilised egg or a seed. What we do is we break up the geode, put the egg inside and assemble it again."

"Egg?" said Lustre succinctly.

"Nascent life form, if you want to be bloody awkward," I snapped in some irritation. "One of those blue bath bubble things you can get in Boots. We just inject a little blob inside."

"I see. And the geode opens up and out comes this … nascent life form," said Lustre testily.

"Sort of," I agreed. "I've thought of a brilliant way to make it look real. What you do, you have the geode, right? Right. You put the film in the camera the other way round, right? Then you roll the bath bubble towards the geode and film that. But when you project the film you put it the right way round and what you see is the bubble rolling towards you. Good, ey?"

"I see" repeated Lustre, patently unimpressed. "And this vessel … if we might call it that … how does it travel to Earth," he added as if addressing a child.

"Well, as a projectile," I parried.

"I see," reiterated Lustre as if overwhelmed with sudden understanding. "And I suppose you have considered the velocity involved against the distance travelled, friction with our atmosphere on entry and impact. And of course, the sophisticated instrumentation, in miniature, inside the … vessel … to regulate … gestation … and determine the time of … birth … or emergence of the well-disposed Alien."

"Wouldn't have to" I explained with conviction. "It would all be done from the Mother Planet. Radio signals."

"Of course," agreed Lustre solemnly. "The calculations involving distance and velocity would need to be very precise, given that the slightest error would result in grave discrepancy given the vast distances involved. I am of course assuming that you would be dealing in Light Years not kilometres."

"Ah, you see? I knew you'd appreciate the need for good science. Make the story credible. Flesh on the bones sort of thing." I tried to sound bright, fearful of mounting annoyance. With Lustre it was hard to tell where innocence ended and sarcasm began.

"As I see it," he continued in lecturing mode "before jumping to any storyline there are matters to be considered in determining the co-efficients relating to distance, velocity, gravitation, temperatures, pressures etc."

"What would that entail, in English?" I queried stretching reasonableness beyond the call of duty.

"To begin with the geode as a projectile is not viable. It's the shape, you see. The roundness. Like Wells' and Lewis' spheres. Not viable. No straight lines. No resistance. Can't maintain shape integrity. You see, depending at what level in matter one were to introduce …" Lustre was obviously going to ramble on. My tether slipped.

"Look here, Lustre," I remonstrated, well out of my pram. "We are talking about a film. A story. Not a string of fucking equations." Lustre appeared to think for a moment, nodding slightly.

"No. Certainly not equations," he said, then adding in his own peculiar fashion, as if thinking aloud "a fucking fairy tale."

Well, that was that. The production stumbled and fell at the first fence. The script never materialised. The little camera, wrapped in black velvet cloth as if in mourning, was consigned to a drawer. Not another word was exchanged between Lustre and myself, as normal indifferences were resumed.

There was little time for brooding as the College went into a period of fervent activity when we were shepherded into alarmingly early applications for admission to the universities of our choice. As expected, Lustre was showered with offers of places at institutions of *venerable stone*. I threw myself at the mercy of Clearance and, given my grades, by-passed *Red Brick* and settled for *concrete block*.

* * * * * * * * *

I ended up in Theology, God knows how. I suspect that at core it was an amalgam of desperation and expediency, as can often be the case with what is later perceived as momentous and life-changing decisions. I had vaguely mused that, having been educated by Christian Brothers with added Altar-serving and choir-singing, I had inside knowledge of the subject. The situation was compounded by dodgey Careers advice and a sales pitch by a Vice-Principal concerned with filling under-subscribed courses, who clinched the deal with vague intimation that it would be possible to make a sideways move to another subject once *on board*.

As it happened I did make a move: not sideways but outwards through the main gates before the end of the first year. It was not a good time for me: not a good time for esoteric discussions on abstract truths. With a singular attack of peeve, I turned my back on all thoughts of a professional career and over the next four years, I sought the reality of working with my hands in factories and Municipal Transport Depots and latterly with my feet as a postal worker.

Inevitably the real reality kicked in, bringing the need to take stock of my situation. Once again, I threw myself at the mercy of a personalised Clearing. It seemed that I was well qualified for the traditional occupations on offer for those of feckless inclination but carrying expectations. Viz: The Church, the Forces and Art. I had 'done' Church in a manner of speaking. The spell in National Service cured any leaning in that direction. That left 'Art'.

A hastily assembled portfolio in which images oozing sentimentality of the Pre Theology Period grated against spiteful cartoons of figures in Clerical garb of the Post Theology Period, was assessed as showing *raw potential* giving me entrance to a Foundation Course. Carried away in a tide where subjective judgements prevail and where ineptness, if vigorously fronted can present as originality, I swirled along a three-year degree course in Fine Art scraping through on a bare Pass, with grazed skin and an aversion to Art.

Returning once again to Clearing, chastened by the admonition that *those who can't … teach,* I lugged out Art Teaching from a depleted barrel. I persisted at the profession for close on twenty years working at full-time Secondary and part-time Adult levels in Evening classes. In its own good time the pique from the Art College experience had gone its merry way, leaving a vacancy. A new tenant took possession. At first it spoke in whispers though insistently. Aware of its rights, the voice became loud and strident hurling accusations of cowardice, fecklessness and terminal procrastination at me. I put up a feeble defence centred around common sense and viability. My arguments were quashed and I had no option but to relent. So at the age of fifty-two, fully equipped with brushes and other instrumentation necessary to give form to unformed ideas, I committed to full-time Art.

I was to occupy that area of activity, strangely, for roughly the same period of time as that of the previous one. Viz: coming up twenty years. I got to thinking that the water was safe and I might venture to where my feet did not touch bottom.

It was then that I found myself caught in an eddy which held me for a time, disorientated and bemused in its swirl before releasing me in a direction which I had not envisaged. I would have expected to have raved, ranted and thrashed about. Instead, I allowed myself to gently drift until, some time after, I felt my feet treading on smooth sand. It appeared that I had arrived at that which presently occupies me: writing. Science Fiction writing, if I am to be believed.

Without knowing it, I was on a path to renewed contact with the now Professor George Lustre and all the irony, poignancy if not tragedy, of the eventual outcome.

Lacking a Science or Engineering background, I struggled at first with a feeling of inadequacy in not being equipped to provide firm grounding for my flights of fancy. I was acutely aware of the world being populated by countless PhDs in the *hard* Sciences able to give a better account of themselves in that respect. But then, the instinct of self-preservation being what it is, I got to thinking that with a different angle of approach together with plausible argument, any deficiency could be seen as an asset. Perhaps my innumerable *qualified* fellows, steeped in their specialisms, might equally be at a disadvantage vis-à-vis the *bigger picture*. OK, there would be need for considerable prevarication on my part in dealing with the specifications of the Proton Drive powering the shuttle to Alpha Centauri in one of my ditties. But I could compensate by my interest in the drive of the day-trippers on board in venturing beyond their world and the implications of a possible encounter with other sentient life.

For when muscle rests and ambition slumbers, is there anything of greater interest, fascination and import than the circumstances of our being and eventual destiny. What has been more than a passing preoccupation may well have accounted for the abrupt ending of the picture-making period from literary overload. Perhaps when the current word-making exhausts itself, there may be a way of returning to picture-making, unbound by literal realism and free to pursue a different reality. As yet there have been no reported sightings of flying pigs.

Fortunately for me, along with the interest in things extra-terrestrials, comes an ingrained wariness of pronouncements from metaphysical or ontological sources. That caution gets sharpened into scepticism when assessing the claims from the host of individuals describing *unearthly* encounters. Of course it is one thing to be sceptical, quite another to be dismissive. The claims are an interesting phenomenon in themselves. There have always been apparitions and encounters with Angels, Devils and Avatars, the form of manifestation in accord with the times and current thinking. It is to be expected that in a time of ferment towards space exploration, the form of the apparitions should be that of Alien beings.

Mankind has always looked upwards with apprehension. Here we stand, in the immensity of an indifferent Universe, beset by two contradictory views of ourselves. On the one hand as mammals with reptilian connections. On the other as divinely-created dispossessed of Paradise and condemned to sweaty toil by the *error of judgement* of one Adam: such as might be claimed, in updated version, by any prominent public personage apprehended in the shrubbery of Hampstead Heath.

And yet, all that dark immensity is not enough to obliterate the glimmer of selfless love and self-sacrifice in humans which would appear to run counter to the ruthless determinants of species survival and to incline more towards a divinity of sorts. We struggle to comprehend, much like a triangle of percussion might in regard to the symphony.

Wishing to compensate for the lack of technical knowledge, I keep one eye open for whatever revelations in astronomy, physics, geology, biology, chemistry etc. are dished out in populist pre-digested form via TV documentaries. I am in the fortunate position of not having to live by the pen or be accountable to any readership other than to a largely sympathetic small circle. Unfettered by specialism I can indulge myself by delving with impunity into the pick-and-mix counter.

My storylines tend never to stray far from US going Thither and THEM coming Hither, always with the question hovering as to what determines human-ness when set against other sentient Intelligences. It's fascinating to imagine how creatures with appreciable levels of technology but of fundamentally different anatomy, physiology and mindset might, in the first place, communicate and then go on to inform each other on such as the origins of Life, beliefs and morality.

Inevitably we come up against the unimaginable since, to a great extent, concepts of Alien sentient beings tend to be extensions of ourselves or, at best, based on evolved strains of other earthly creatures: invariably insects. For on these we can ascribe qualities of relentless collective industry without the hindrance of emotional complications at the individual level. It would be interesting to conjure up sentient Beings of humanoid aspect, but not subject to the three 'S's of Sex (procreation), Sustenance (fuel) and Sleep (regeneration).

These speculations hold well and good as material in Science Fiction, for as yet we haven't encountered extra-terrestrial Life. Not so in the case of setting foot on the Moon. In that regard we could say *Houston we have a problem*. In fact the problem is Houston. Not in itself but as part of the Space Programme. It is to do with something not uncommon in human affairs generally:

the need to temper the thrill of the long-held anticipation with the comparative banality of the eventual reality. Romance making room for pragmatism.

H.G. Wells' Mr Cavor blithely steps on to the Lunar Surface, into breathable air, and forthwith engages in heroic *Boys' Adventure* escapades with the subterranean insectile Selenites. NASA's envoys on the other hand, encumbered by the accoutrements for survival, find little by way of diversion other than floating jumps and the odd game of very handicapped mock golf.

Then there's the character of the respective Moon Landers. We have the rubicon Mr Cavor, cast in the very British mould of genteel eccentricity, brilliant of mind but emotionally impaired, presumably as a result of a Public School education. In contrast we have the Astronauts of fighter-pilot credentials, in the prime of physical condition and cleared for psychological and emotional stability.

Hence to the preparations for lift-off. In the case of Mr Cavor it involves putting the cat out, leaving a note for the milkman, making sure everything is turned off and leaving the front door key under the mat. Chances are that, true to character, he will be wearing odd socks and will have forgotten to pack a toothbrush. Quite a different order of magnitude to that of the countdown for Apollo, with the complexity and precision of the vast technical support.

As to the trip itself, there's Mr Cavor in sole charge of regulating the trajectory approach and landing. He does so by the expedient of rolling and unrolling a blind inside his home-made sphere. The blind is compounded of the substance Cavorite which acts counter to the exertion of gravity. If only life was so simple for the multitude in Ground Control in managing the banks of computers monitoring every aspect of the Mission.

No amount of frivolous wise-cracking can, nor is it intended to belittle or detract from the dedication and achievement of all involved in the Space Programme. Certainly not from the valour of those who sit atop a bomb to be blasted off at neck-compressing velocity.

If anything it is a shot across the bows of the work of Science Fiction writers, or indeed writers in general. Does it invite a false view of reality with false expectations, or can it be validated in firing imagination and optimism towards ideals?

We can identify with the Cavors if only because they are individuals. We can share their enthusiasms because they haven't been swallowed by the machinations of vast enterprises supported by a budget with the potential to bankrupt a Nation.

When I decided to renew contact with George Lustre, curiosity apart, I was prompted by ulterior motive on two counts. One concerned a particular piece which I was working on. The other involved the purchase of a microscope. As far as the writing went, it was the old thing of seeking validation from a Science viewpoint, much as I had with that film script which never materialised.

I thought the theme for my story carried a certain originality of approach, while being plagued by the notion that I must have come across it in the work of some established Science Fiction writer. However, I ploughed on telling myself that there were only a handful of themes around and what distinguished a work was the treatment. (I am here reminded of a pithy quote on the scarcity of themes. It related to Opera: ... *there is only one story. The tenor wants to give the soprano one and the baritone won't let him).*

There were strands in the idea which, if properly brought together, touched on the possibility of the existence of extra-terrestrial Sentient Life while at the same time pointing to the improbability of contact, given the prohibitive distances and time scales involved. I was determined to steer clear of travel in suspended animation; aboard Eco systems for generations and the imploded tunnels of Black Holes. Instead, I allowed myself one vital assumption. It was that the Human species, currently in its infancy if measured on what might be the Geological Scale, survived to enjoy a span on a par with that of the Dinosaurs. For it would require that very generous time scale for the scenario of the story to be viable and for the Law of Chance to operate. (The Law states that given sufficient time it is possible for a chimpanzee to type out the complete works of Shakespeare. The Law goes into improbability in regard to being selected to be selected to take part in the Readers' Digest Prize Draw).

Our descendants are then free to continue to exercise the instinct to colonise and duly populate a scatter of far-flung stars, each isolated and ignorant of each other's existence. As would be expected, over the aeons, the insidious forces of gravity, atmosphere and terrain would alter the physiology, anatomy and psychology of the colonisers in adaptation.

In the fullness of time, a convoy from Earth chances on one such sidereal settlement where the newly-arrived have an encounter of the startling kind with the locals. Although strange in many ways to the eyes of the incomers, these have basically similar configuration of physique and disposition of limbs. But there ends the similarity with great disparity in language, behaviour, culture, customs and beliefs. The Star People have legends and songs. They tell of the ache of a yearning for green fields and blue waters: of returning to Old Mother Terra.

The microscope connection did not directly relate to the writing. Peering through the lens of my own instrument had been on the 'Must Do' list for some time. It rose on the list as the available time for doing so fell. I had been reluctant to acquire a model which might give a magnification not so far removed from that of a good magnifying glass and sadly a Scanning Electron version was out of reach. So, with necessity being in some way related to compromise, I had reached the point of settling for the best model I could sensibly afford.

The spark which re-ignited the long-smouldering embers came with the news that yet another smaller particle had been discovered by the means of collisions accelerated to the speed of Light.

Once again overawed by the physics, I scurried to the safety of the metaphysical, there to ponder the possibility that the sub-divisions in matter might be subject to the Infinite, such as with Space and Time. Or alternatively that a point might be reached where quantity becomes quality: that being the Volition at the centre of the thrust to Life.

Put simply, I wanted a microscope for two reasons. The first was to experience at first hand the spaces within what appears to be solid, the other to similarly experience the commotion in apparent stillness. With that in mind, I would need an instrument which allowed the viewing of objects as well as slides. It was on those lines that I questioned George Lustre over the phone, not that I got any answers.

* * * * * * * * *

My train pulled into Paddington on time. I had no difficulty in spotting George Lustre as he scanned the disgorged passengers with eager bird-like movements of his head. Once past the barriers, I stood in front of him, which had the effect of making him blink furiously whilst peering at me.

"It is, isn't it?" he finally spluttered, obviously penetrating the unfamiliar beard, glasses and grey hairs.

"Professor Lustre, I presume," I countered in mock historical.

"Yes, yes of course, certainly," assented Lustre and we both engaged in a series of abortive handshakes and awkward quasi-salutes, before settling for reciprocal beams.

"Er, shall we go?" queried Lustre, turning abruptly and starting to walk. I fell in step. "It's the Underground, I fear. District Line to Upminster. It's the parking, you see." He pointed ahead and we went down some steps to the trains.

He hadn't changed much apart from a slight stoop and some loss of hair. What was left of it had an orangey red tinge which, perhaps unjustly, I put down to henna and which accentuated the extreme pallor of his face. He seemed to me to have that peculiar brightness of eye and dilated nostrils of someone battling fatigue or sleep deprivation. He was dressed in careless manner: brown cords, salt-and-pepper tweed jacket, none-too-white shirt, crumpled black tie and incongruous white plimsolls.

In Upminster we drew out of a car park in an old maroon Ford. The next stage of the journey was a nightmare of sudden swerves, drastic braking at red lights, lunges from green, hair-raising over-taking and stalling at a roundabout. Acutely aware of my predicament I was careful not to engage in idle chatter, not wishing to further endanger life by distracting the obviously stressed driver.

In the fullness of time, we came to semi-rural land with a scatter of detached houses and a sign which welcomed us to South Ockendon exhorting us, somewhat belatedly, to drive carefully. We turned into what I judged to be an estate of post-war Council houses and drew up outside one, numbered thirty-eight. A wrestle with a dilapidated gate, considerable fumbling at the front door and we entered. Journey's end.

Once my eyes adjusted to the musty gloom, I found myself in a narrow hallway of walls painted half cream half brown, bare floorboards and a staircase. Lustre fumbled for a wall switch. A dismal *click* delivered nothing other than an irritable *Tch* from Lustre, who promptly vanished. A lurid light appeared along the hallway to my right and towards it I went like a bemused moth.

It came from a room off the hallway where I found Lustre grappling with one of two light fittings in the recesses on the sides of a stone fireplace. The extra light added to the meagre wattage of the bare bulb dangling on twisted brown flex from the ceiling, revealing a room of Spartan sparseness comprising two armchairs, a coffee table and a Valour gas heater of simulated logs. The theme of bare boards persisted.

"I don't use certain parts of the house," said my host. "Only the kitchen and, of course, upstairs for the bathroom and bedroom. I spend most of my time in my workroom … oh, I've made ready the back bedroom for you.

"Thanks," I said and then "I had formed the idea that you had a large house."

"Oh no no no. Yes. Well when my parents were alive. I got this place in the eighties. Thatcher era when Council Houses were sold off."

"I see," I said, although I couldn't. "Suited you, did it?"

"Oh most definitely. There was the space at the back and the long path of course. But the main thing was the direct line of connection with Estonia, you see." I still couldn't see but I had more pressing needs.

"Could I use the bathroom?" I asked. "I'd like to freshen up after the journey." My words fell on deaf ears for Lustre, after an abrupt movement of his head stared pensively at the ceiling.

"It's upstairs is it?" I said slightly raising my voice in the manner of a polite cough to attract attention.

"Oh – what?" Lustre said irritably after another of his head movements.

"The bathroom," I repeated. "It's upstairs isn't it?"

"Oh yes. Upstairs. Yes. Certainly." Lustre favoured me with a smile of mild satisfaction as might someone returning from somewhere nice. Still wearing my overcoat and carrying my overnight bag, I returned to the hallway. I found a light switch at the base of the staircase which rewarded me with light on the landing above. I could then make out an array of vacant hooks on the wall where I hung my coat and I rested my bag on the floor beneath it. I made my way upstairs somewhat disconcerted by the intrusion on the hollow silence from my shoes on bare wood.

On reaching the landing I opened the door directly facing the stairs and pulled on a cord switch.

I took a sharp involuntary breath. If the room downstairs, and indeed what I had seen of the house, could be described as shabby, here was *sumptuous*. The wall which held the door and the one opposite, glowed in a lustrous green which in my days among paint tubes I would have described as Viridian. To my right, the entire wall from ceiling to floor was draped in elegant folds of a rich ruby plush, echoed by a luxurious wall-to-wall carpet. In contrast, the wall to my left was a bank of electronic equipment, among which I could only identify an impressive stereo sound system, several computers and an oscilloscope. Among the proliferation of glass and chrome one object caught my attention: a metronome. One whole shelf was given over to a collection of CDs, tapes and video cassettes.

A faint tinkling drew my gaze upwards to a ceiling of Cerulean blue from which hung a many-tiered chandelier. In the centre of the room, facing the equipment, stood a podium with a brass rail and a music stand. Behind it was an ornate chair. Draped over its back was a jacket, emerald green, in what appeared to be velvet. On the seat of the chair, also upholstered in rich ruby, rested a conductor's baton.

I found the bathroom and refreshed, made my way downstairs, where I found Lustre sitting on one of the armchairs apparently lost in thought. I stifled my curiosity about the room upstairs. Instead, rubbing my hands together, I let drop an appreciable hint.

"That's better," I enthused. "A nice cup of tea and I'll be right as rain." If by that I expected Lustre to jump to his feet and offer copious apology for his shortcomings as host, I was mistaken.

"Oh dear," he said in that peculiar way as to himself. "Tea? I only take water." Going by the way he had spoken on the phone and now by his behaviour, it was obvious that my erstwhile friend inhabited a universe in which the laws of practicalities and social niceties did not apply. It seemed that if I were to keep body and soul together during my stay, I would need to take matters in hand. As yet I had no inkling of what was expected of me. Lustre had not exactly been forthcoming about his circumstances and I was puzzled as to how I could be of help, given that he knew nothing or showed the slightest interest in my situation. The man was obviously involved in something which totally absorbed him and left room for very little else. Until I knew what was expected of me, I could at least take on the role of mother hen cum schoolmaster.

"So," I beamed in brisk pleasantness. "Whereabouts is your kitchen?"

"Er, along the hallway." Lustre remained seated. Wondering what other encounters might come my way, I found a switch which lit up what might be the kitchen if the butler sink, electric kettle, cooker, microwave and fridge were anything to go by. It didn't take long to deduce that therein meandered a bachelor and vegetarian: moreover an extremely frugal one. Either that or he had a housekeeper going by the name of Old Mother Hubbard.

I strode back to where Lustre still sat tugging at his bottom lip.

"Are there any shops nearby?" I asked placing myself in front of him, causing another of his furious blinking spells.

"Yes, yes of course, certainly. In the village," he said as if returning from somewhere but not quite sure where he was.

"Walking distance?" I pressed. Vigorous nodding by the interrogated. "Left or right out of the house?"

"Oh right … I mean left."

"I shan't be long." On the way out I picked up my coat.

I found a convenience store where I bought some bread and since Man does not live by bread alone, tea, coffee, butter, sugar, milk, marmalade, cereals, eggs, bacon, cooking oil, baked beans, salami, olives, Jaffa cakes, pink wafers, and two reasonable bottles of wine, red and white. I thought I'd better get screw-tops, just in case. The shopkeeper was only too willing to call me a taxi and I returned to number thirty eight.

Making sure Lustre was still where I'd left him, I went straight to the kitchen, laid out a reasonable cold supper on the kitchen table and put the shopping away. Lustre appeared in the doorway and seemed to hesitate. Without speaking, I pointed to a chair and took one myself.

Mine host politely declined to join me at the table. He explained, if explanation it was, that he needed to be in his workroom since he would be leaving for Estonia which only left tomorrow to sort things out. As an afterthought he said my bedroom was the one overlooking the back; to feel free to occupy it at any time of my choosing and that in the morning we would make a start. With that he scuttled along the passage-way. I heard a door open and shut and bolts being slipped. I opened the red and set to, bewildered and not a little bothered.

I don't usually go to bed before midnight. However, you couldn't describe the day as 'usual', so at around ten, in the absence of the TV with the possibility of a late night film, I made my way upstairs. My room was little more than a box-room but the single bed seemed comfortable and clean enough. I sat on the bed with that hollow indecisive feeling I get in hotel rooms when the only option appears to be to drift off and wake with a start. I was well into a sequence when I became aware of a regular sound. It seemed to be coming from outside. Instinctively I put my light out and went over to the window. The sound was coming from footsteps. Although the night was clouded over, there was no mistaking the figure of Lustre walking, away from me, along a straight path. The path ended at a hedge, where Lustre turned and walked back in my direction. I must have watched him do at least ten laps before my eyelids rebelled and I was glad to 'call it a day'.

I woke early. Washed and dressed, I reminded myself that I was in a self-catering establishment and quietly went downstairs in search of breakfast. There was no sign of Lustre. When into my second cup of coffee, the morning's stillness was disturbed by the abrupt sliding of a bolt followed by the opening and closing of a door along the hallway. Presently Lustre appeared in the doorway to the kitchen, looking rather the worse for wear.

"Morning," I greeted in guest-brightness. "Can I get you something?"

"Oh hello. No no no. I'm quite fine." He sounded impatient or perhaps just plain tired.

"I'll just finish my coffee and do a quick clear-up." As I spoke I pointed to a chair. After some hesitation Lustre came over and sat down. I had no intention of hurrying. In fact I was quietly determined to get some answers, if only out of curiosity. "Enjoyed your stroll in the back last night?" I posed as an opener.

"Oh yes yes most definitely. Very beneficial even in the absence of stars. A necessary part of my schedule, you see," he replied rather abstractly.

"Schedule?" Oh yes, I needed some answers. I was on the hunt.

"Well yes yes. My time is fully occupied and I need to keep to a strict schedule if I am to maintain a healthy balance," he said as if stating the obvious.

"Balance?" I said. Instincts told me that I might best penetrate his habitual reticence by prods echoing his own words.

"Oh yes yes. Along with intellectual engagement there needs to be proportionate periods given to exercise, relaxation and reflection. In my case I have ascertained the optimum benefit to derive from two periods each of twenty eight minutes duration. You will notice that although giving three elements, namely exercise, relaxation and reflection, I have allotted only two periods of twenty-eight minutes each. That is because I've been able to combine exercise with reflection and exercise with relaxation." My curiosity was approaching critical level. I would have to draw out my coffee.

"Combine?" Another prod, taking a pretend sip.

"Oh yes yes. My stroll, as you put it quite inaccurately if I may say. With reflection certainly. Most certainly. It's in the pacing, you see. It must accord with the level of activity of your thoughts so that it comes automatically. The pacing that is. Then it allows for reflection. Most useful in putting the work in perspective, you see. Also, perhaps more significantly it throws up pointers towards future progress, you see. Most pleasant on a starry night. Most inspiring. Glimpse of the infinite, as it were."

"I see. And the relaxation part?"

"Oh, on the same lines. Exercise combined with music. I have a suitable room upstairs."

"Oh?"

"Yes yes. I do a spot of conducting, you see." There was a tumble inside my head as green walls, red carpets and drapes, green jackets, podiums, conductors' batons and chandeliers crashed through.

"Oh. You have a group?"

"No no no. I conduct to recorded music."

"Oh. You've studied music?"

"Oh no. Not in the accepted sense. I transcribe known pieces into a system involving tempo, interval and variation."

"Do you have favourite composers?"

"Oh no. Although I will concede that classical orchestral music in general best suits my purpose. I find that popular music tends to keep to a persistent level of tempo, going into the repetitive and lacking the variations in symphonic music."

"I don't understand," I puzzled. "Are you saying that you conduct to your own transcription of an original piece? To your own re-recording?"

"Not at all. My transcription is merely a means of selecting suitable pieces."

"Suitable?"

"Yes, as I have explained, in terms of variations in tempo and vigour. I conduct the pieces as originally composed."

"But how, if as you say, you have not studied music?"

"Ah, you've heard of the persistence of vision. You've done some film-making if I remember rightly. Well there is also what we might call persistence of hearing."

"Oh?"

"You appear to imply that by a lack of technical knowledge of a particular piece or indeed of music generally one would conduct out of synchronisation, lagging behind, aping what had gone before."

"Well …."

"If so you would be incorrect, although strictly speaking not so. I will grant you that there would be a discrepancy between my hearing and my movements in conducting. But it would register in milliseconds. And because one is reacting to the sound in reflex as you might say, much like the pacing for my reflection and given the persistence of hearing, there would be an overlap and to all intents and purposes one would be conducting in time with the music." Even if the theory held water it did not explain the sumptuousness of that room. It was the card up my sleeve. I had to be careful how I played it without letting on that I had prior knowledge. My curiosity was well above clinical level. Time for another prod.

"I see. So in essence you simply play a selected piece and conduct to it, getting your exercise and at the same time letting the music work its magic and relax you." I deliberately sought to expose the bare bones and it worked.

"Not entirely," half-snapped Lustre. There was definitely, if not wounded, offended pride in the tone. "You see, given the required result it is necessary to provide a sympathetic ambience."

"Ambience?" Prod, prod.

"Well yes. The décor of the surroundings."

"Décor?"

"Well yes. In terms of vibrations emanating from colours and textures."

"Colours?"

"The predominant colour needed to be green. Not any green of course. One which tended towards the blue spectrum with a counterpoint of red similarly inclined. There is one indulgence in the form of a chandelier. It belonged to my mother. A family heirloom. As a little boy I used to love its tingling sound when opening the front door caused a draught." No mention of the jacket. That green jacket. Therein lay the flaw in the science. Anyway, enough was enough. There was no need to be unkind. I switched off the prod. I took a sip of coffee. Stone cold. Worth it though.

"Shall we make a start," said Lustre in a changed voice, rising abruptly to his feet.

We went along the hallway to what appeared to be an extension to the original building. Lustre unlocked a reinforced door. We entered. He bolted the door on the inside. With indecisive flicker, fluorescent tubes lit up.

You couldn't call it a room. Not with a ceiling well over fifteen feet high to my estimation and no windows. I wasn't surprised at all the paraphernalia which goes to make up a workroom/laboratory/office and part living quarters. What stunned me was the cube. Going by the average height of a man, it must have been over ten feet high. It was featureless and presented in dull gun-metal grey. I must have been gawping at it.

"Ah. The figuration," said Lustre as in complete explanation, not to say justification, of the monstrosity.

"Figuration?"

"Yes. Optimum figuration for re-figuration," further elucidated Lustre.

"I see," I said in exhalation with all the conviction of a mole with cataracts surfacing into fog.

"You see," continued Lustre, piling on the intended explanation and putting the top hat on my bewilderment, "it's constructed to a factor of six from twelve. It's the necessary configuration with resistance to maintain integrity. A sphere wouldn't do. No no no. Definitely wouldn't do at all. Would be integrated in the confluence, as it were."

"Confluence?" I found a stool and sat down. "Lustre, would you mind telling me in a way I can understand, what all this is about? And what part I am expected to play in it?"

"Oh, a very important part, I assure you," said Lustre, nodding in a curious manner then adding in that peculiar way of his as if thinking aloud, "Essential, I would say. At this stage of the link-up certainly. Most certainly. With Estonia."

"Estonia?" I bleated. "Lustre, please sit down. What is that cube thing?" With some reluctance, Lustre picked up a folding chair and sat facing me.

"My dear fellow," he said with little shakes of his head. "I rather fear you would be adverse to the f.......... *equations*, if my memory serves me well. Besides, I leave for Estonia in the morning and if you are to familiarise yourself with the activating procedure, we should begin at once." With that he rose abruptly and went over to a large console with a bewildering array of LEDs, switches, plungers, dials, levers, sliding equalisers, rheostats and the like. He waited for me to follow him. I remained seated.

"If it involves that thing" I said, pointing to the console. "Why don't you employ a technician? What if I foul up?"

"Oh, you mustn't. Most definitely not," said Lustre aghast. "As for the technician, it's the science, you see. One mustn't disclose until the science is proven and one can publish. I can rely on your discretion, you see."

"Lustre," I intoned school-masterly. "Return to your chair. Start at the beginning. It will be quicker in the long run, believe me. You don't want to be plagued with ceaseless questions."

"Yes, I do see," he said to my surprise, returning to his seat. He inhaled slowly and continued, his voice distant. "I've been working on refiguration for well over thirty years. Since I graduated in fact. In fact, I do believe the germ of the idea came in the Sixth Form. Remember we talked about Wells and Lewis and the viability of the sphere? I held a lecturing position but my research into refiguration has been conducted in strict privacy. My parents left considerable assets, which enabled me to resign and commit full-time to research. I was able to get construction work on the building done and of course gather all the equipment necessary for the work in the laboratory. One had to be circumspect about the materials and assembly of the cube, as also about its intended use. The labour I employed came with impeccable credentials. There was also extensive laying of ..."

"When I saw you in The Sky at Night then," I interrupted, "presumably you were not discussing your work here."

"Oh good gracious me. No no no. It related to consultancy work I had undertaken on propulsion."

I struggled. Lustre struggled. I to comprehend. He to explain. Time and again I interrupted him whilst in full flow of technicalities. Time and again he groped for analogies, metaphors and comparables, as lost in the attempt as I was in the science. At times he appeared in despair, whether to find the words or from a reluctance to do so, I couldn't tell. What I did learn I had to piece together, often by insistence. Other times, although lost myself, I had but to allow him full rein. Such was the fervour which transformed him. If I might here intrude with my own thoughts, during those times I felt as if listening to some unknown symphonic piece: moved without needing to understand. I needed to suspend incredulity: to level my confusion at my own shortcomings.

As far as I was able to comprehend and now retain, here are the bare bones, complete with gaping holes. The analogy which I use as a starting point to Lustre's proposition is my own.

A valued object is to be sent from A to B. It is consigned to the driver of a vehicle and transported in a container along a thoroughfare. Lustre proposed to effect the delivery whilst eliminating the need for driver, vehicle and indeed for the road itself. He did however stress the need for *the* container. Trying to keep a handle on the tangible I suggested, in facetious manner, the alternative of pilot, plane and airways. The quip was received with icy disapproval and the terse retort of there being *other pathways and means of conveyancing*. Abashed, I sought to redeem myself by alluding, in what I hoped was an informed tone, to electrical currents and radio waves. This incurred violent disapproval from Lustre with dismissive gestures. I was obviously treading on Holy Ground and I though it prudent, if I was going to get anywhere, to remove my sandals. However, my obvious ignorance appeared to goad him to greater effort in making me understand. It was then he dropped the bombshell.

He intended to send a *valued object*, already inside that massive cube, from the cube to Estonia *by means of refiguration*.

While I busied myself in coping with my dazed condition, Lustre beamed at me with schoolboy glee. I managed to drag myself as close to coherence as to be able to croak: "You mean? … actually … without? … only by? … Estonia?" Then it got difficult for me as Lustre went into specifics.

I was told that the cube conformed to the strict dimensions of 12'x12'x12'. Constructed to what he described as a factor of 6 from 12, these being the elements for optimum refiguration. Twelve layers of special materials made up the walls of the cube, giving an internal space of precisely 6'x6'x6'. Apparently a complex network of cables, pipes and vents run under the concrete floor connecting the inner cube to the console.

Inside the inner cube defiguration took place. According to Lustre, this entailed reducing the object to its integral sub-atomic components. These would be *emitted* to an *Inducer* in Estonia where the object would undergo refiguration. Lustre explained, if explanation it was, that the integrity of figuration of the object was maintained by the resistance of the cube to assimilation within the confluence in emission.

If I understood the gist of the considerable mouthful, it meant that my friend was about to send, or attempt to send an object, which he stressed as being valuable, from South Ockendon to Estonia by means unfamiliar to the haulage business.

That considerable feat apart, why Estonia one might ask, which I did. The answer I received was, in its way, as puzzling as the science itself: it seems that Lustre, of all people, went to Estonia for the Eurovision Song Contest when it was being hosted there. I felt loathe to probe further in that direction fearing it to be the area also occupied by the green velvet jacket. I was content with the explanation that whilst there, Lustre saw opportunities in terms of available properties, seclusion and skilled labour so as to further his research. Over the years he had divided his time between South Ockendon in Essex and Estonia.

Delivered of that enticing morsel of information, Lustre shook his head as might a dog to dispel wetness and rose abruptly from his seat. He scurried over to the console to where he beckoned impatiently that I should follow. Having neither the breath nor the will to resist, I also rose and went zombie-like and glazed of eye, towards the console. There I was formally introduced to every blessed item on that board together with parentage and function. I listened to his voice which appeared to be coming from a great distance and as such registered as a lulling drone. Sharp sound intruded on my reverie. Lustre was violently tapping a clipboard, which found its way into my nervous grip. With some effort, I managed to dispel images of green jackets and euphoric cavortings, to focus on the clipboard. Bold letters double-underlined stated 'Sequence of Operation', followed by a list of mercifully succinct instructions. Although these were of admirable clarity and simplicity, Lustre was insistent on numerous dry runs. I lost count of the number but finally he appeared satisfied with my competence.

There followed some final, most explicit, verbal instructions. I was to activate the sequence at precisely 10.04 the next morning by the clock on the console. I was to remain at the console, with my mobile fully charged, to receive his call from Estonia. He would be catching an overnight flight.

I was at the console well before nine o'clock, going over the Operation Schedule again and again, like some over-rehearsed actor. For a time I amused myself with counting to the rhythm of the flashing seconds on the digital clock of the console. Then I strolled around the labyrinth of equipment, apparatus, workbenches and less identifiable objects. I was careful not to wander too close to the cube.

9.27. Back at the console I flicked idly through my notebook. I had hopes of using the time productively. No words came. I positioned and repositioned my mobile. Went for another stroll.

10.0.   Back at the console again, I gave my palms a final wipe and curled the fingers of my right hand round the black handle of the lever which would initiate the sequence. At the precise instant of 10.04.00 I pulled it smoothly towards me; flicked the three switches; set Equaliser A to 10; set Equaliser B to 2; waited for the 'Start' button to flash green; pressed down on it; closed my eyes tightly. I became aware of a slight tremor underfoot. A smell I recognised twitched my nostrils. It took me to the seaside. I opened my eyes. I couldn't see any difference in the cube.

My tension started to ease as I consciously made myself relax. There was nothing else for me to do but wait for Lustre's phone call. Having no idea when that would come, I once again flicked through my notebook to the last page with writing and took out my pen. Then my mobile buzzed.

I snatched it.

"Yes … Lustre? … how was it?" I blurted out.

"Quite satisfactory," said the thin voice. "I should be back by early evening." Silence.

"Hello hello. Lustre." He had switched off.

* * * * * * * * *

The muffled sound of a car door closing. *Lustre.* Gratefully laying down my pen, I quickly downed the rest of the red in the tumbler and hurried to open the front door.

Lustre was having his contre-temps with the gate. He looked up and raised a finger in greeting. "I have something to show you," he called out, coming along the path. Once inside the house, he led the way to the kitchen. With one hand he set aside my pad and tumbler, with the other he carefully rested the seasoned attaché case which he carried on the kitchen table. He released the clasps, one at a time, and paused. Then as if performing a ritual, he opened the case using the middle finger of each hand. With utmost care, using two hands, he lifted out an object loosely wrapped in black velvet which he rested on the table. Again another pause before he proceeded to undo the folds, smoothing each on the table as he did so. An ornate silver photograph frame stood revealed.

Lustre took a step back and looked at me. Leaning forward I looked at the photograph within the frame. It showed an imperious woman in her middle years. I looked at Lustre.

"My mother," he announced with triumph in his voice, then "it's the object I sent to Estonia." I sat down.

"Are you telling me that you placed this frame inside the cube in your workroom and … retrieved … it … in Estonia?" I said, just above a whisper.

"Quite so," agreed Lustre and set about the ritual in reverse, finally picking up the attaché case. "I'll just return it to its place upstairs." I remained seated, somewhat dazed, faintly registering footsteps, doors opening or closing, the cistern flushing.

"I do hope you don't mind me disappearing." Lustre stood in the kitchen doorway. "Really I should see to things in the workroom," adding in that peculiar way of his "much to be done. Much work to be done."

"Lustre," I half-shouted, perhaps inappropriately. "Get yourself in here and sit down." I myself got up and went over to the fridge.

"Do you begin to realise what you've just told me?" I gasped. "You have sent/transmitted/emitted whatever, a solid object God knows how from one part of the Globe to another. What's more …"

At that point words failed me. For his part, either taken aback or simply plain embarrassed by my little outburst, Lustre approached the table. He put up no resistance when I pressed on his shoulders and sat him down.

"Even if you don't appear to appreciate what you have done," I continued. "I do and I intend to celebrate that achievement. What's more, you are going to join me if only out of politeness towards a guest in your house." With that, I fetched two tumblers from the cupboard above the sink and plonked them on the table. I opened the white and after filling the tumblers handed one to Lustre and raised the other.

"I couldn't possibly …" began Lustre.

"Please yourself" I interrupted. "I intend to celebrate. If I can't do it with you, you leave me no option but to do it with somebody else."

"Oh no no. That is not possible. Most certainly not at all desirable," gasped Lustre all aflutter. "Perhaps we might. Just this once. Special occasion."

"To a remarkable and unique achievement" I said in all sincerity and emptied my tumbler. Lustre stood as if frozen. I glared at him. He took a sip. Savoured the wine and took another sip. He gave a little sideways nod and reaching for the bottle, began reading the back label.

"Lustre," I admonished. "It's a celebratory drink. That's all you need to know. Enjoy it."

"Quite so," agreed Lustre and drained his tumbler.

"Well," I said. "We might as well do this thing properly. Here, take one of these." I held out the opened packet of pink wafers I'd been nibbling on as an aid to concentration. "Go on. Take one. No need to read the packet. It's suitable for Vegetarians." He took one with a near-smile as I refilled his tumbler.

When in time the wafers were reduced to pink dust on silver paper and the bottle depleted of content, Lustre rose unsteadily from the table. An inane grin gave his features a look of pleasant surprise. Gathering resolve, he traced a tangent to the kitchen doorway and with a series of ricochets along the passageway, achieved purchase on the banister. From thence, after drawing breath, he proceeded up the stairs with sustained heaving on the handrail. "Most enjoyable. Most enjoyable," he kept repeating in uncharacteristically loud tone. I lingered awhile and after my customary cup of strong black coffee before turning in, followed in his wake.

* * * * * * * * *

I was glad of the long return journey home by train. There was much to reflect on: much to absorb during that interval of suspension between departures and arrivals. I retained an image of Lustre waving diffidently at chest level and then, with hand and head lowered, disappearing indoors before my taxi was out of sight.

His manner together with the outmoded clothes and incongruous white plimsolls belied that something of the heroic in him. A latter day Cavor, he carried his eccentricities as shield and, perhaps more significantly, as reliable signposts in the uncharted terrain of his exploration. Along with achievement, along with the exhilaration and exultation of a pursuit demanding total absorption, his stooped shoulders also bore the weight of his exclusion from the sustaining warmth of human interaction.

On the day of my departure he appeared willing, at times eager, to converse. Time and again he referred to much work needing to be done, in that way of his as to himself. As delicately as I could, I managed at one point to steer the conversation towards the framed photograph of his mother. I was curious about it being the object selected for the first trial within the cube. The explanation given was that *the object embodied disparate substances: metal, glass, card, as well as residual chemicals from the processing of the photograph.* He became animated and appeared at pains to emphasize that *the object had not incurred damage either superficially or in the integrity of its internal structure.* This appeared to give him the greatest satisfaction in the entire enterprise.

He spoke of the *limitation of the inducer and the need for variable location.* He said that it presented his most pressing concern. As I was given to understand, as things stood he could only operate between the cube and Estonia. By *variable location* he meant other locations in addition to that in Estonia. I was flummoxed with visions of Lustre capering around the globe snapping up cheap property. Then he delivered another of his winding blows.

Apparently it was theoretically possible to actually emit the inducers themselves to chosen locations. The concept went over my head but I was assured that the science was sound and that all that was required was *a shift in the source of propulsion.* My nit-picking query regarding limits in the distances involved was brushed aside with a vague gesture. He became abstracted. His eyes seemed to glaze over.

"You know, Foyle" he said as from a distance. "I was brought up R.C. Mother was very devout. You know, this dissolution and re-arranging of particles, trans-substantiation if you like, is not a new notion. It is one of the duties of Science to discover old truths. Old truths, new Science. The challenge, Foyle, is in dealing with the components of organic matter. You see, anything which exists, from rocks to thoughts, has substance. It is simply a question of penetrating the level at which it vibrates. We can, as I have shown, manipulate the components of inert matter. Imagine then that level of understanding applied to organic, even sentient matter. Imagine the possibility of organising, reconstituting or replacing its components. It would simply be a question of complexity. Resurrection would take on new meaning. Old truths, new Science."

* * * * * * * * *

In the first few weeks after returning home, I made numerous phone calls to Lustre. Having become acquainted with his situation, I did have some concerns about his well-being. However, I failed to make contact. My calls were met by discordant high pitched sound or else by numb buzzing. On the single occasion when I heard the ringing tone, it just went on interminably and I lost patience. I chose to allay my concern with the thought that he might prefer his privacy respected.

I was myself having a difficult time work-wise. The piece I was attempting to get to grips with, which I had ambitiously titled 'Second Coming' had fallen flat, appearing fatuous, hackneyed and self-indulgent. Again that thing, exacerbated by the Lustre experience, of the writing lacking informed reinforcement. I felt the idea to have a kernel of substance, I just lacked the equipment to penetrate the husk of banality. I was, you might say, merrily driving along on what I would call 'abdominal intuition' only to discover that when I needed to apply the brakes of the 'rational', I found them faulty. It was time, once again, to go to Clearing.

In an attempt at the positive, I finally bought myself the long-desired microscope: a Zenith Ultra-500 LA with magnifications of x40x100x400x1000.

There followed a period of engrossed peering out of which came the idea for the possible use of the marbles.

I should explain that some years previously when I was trying my hand at 3D work with cardboard, as a result of another option from Clearing, I had the notion to buy 6000 beautiful translucent Cobalt blue marbles. Needless to say, I was assailed by constant jibes of 'at least chances are you won't ever lose all your marbles'. However there was a kind of logic for what might appear as an impulse purchase of singular and unaccountable capriciousness.

In 1984 when Art Teaching was suggested at Clearing, I took part in a school project. In essence it involved starting with the dot, as the smallest mark, and by magnification, proliferation and disposition, reproduce in precise detail a larger version of a continuous tone, much smaller, original image.

The marbles were envisaged as 3 Dimensional versions of the dots and used as simple basic units to arrive at a complex structure. Curiously when peering through the lenses the idea presented not so much from the configurations revealed as from the spaces between them. It was time to invest in 6000 clear marbles to add to the blues. In order to squeeze a little extra mileage from the little spheres before them being bonded into some bizarre construction, a further idea came a-knocking. Further, it involved collaboration with a photographer who, unlike me, was computer literate. Although fairly comfortable with photography at the 'wet processing' level, the 'dry digital' is a closed book for me. In any case, I preferred the idea of someone with more specialised savvy to do the clicking, leaving me to play my part with the marbles, as it were.

The objective was to photograph the marbles against various blue backgrounds using spot/diffused/strobe lighting, from different viewpoints and using the techniques of time/high speed and multiple exposures plus animation.

The marbles were to be arranged singly and in clusters in a variety of configurations and expanse: dropped and bounced against hard and yielding surface; rolled down from inclines through blue paint; dropped into water and wallpaper paste; animated into forming shapes etc. etc. The images obtained would then be manipulated digitally. Whereas I recoil at computer generated images, I have no problem with enhancing or accentuating original images of my own with a specific aim in view.

In setting out the foregoing rigmarole of I thought this, I thought that and I did the other, I continue to try to convince myself that I had been a busy little bee. That as such, I might wring out a reason or excuse for not persevering in trying to contact Lustre. Not that had I succeeded, I might have been able to avert the outcome. Even if I had any inkling of what that might be. Foresight gives but limited vision, in contrast to the 20/20 acuity of hindsight.

* * * * * * * * *

The news came four years after my visit to Lustre at his home. A large envelope. Recorded delivery. I was having a coffee break in the kitchen at the time and to there I returned. Too curious to sit down again, I opened the envelope. Inside was a two-page letter from a Firm of Solicitors with an address in Hornchurch, Essex. Attached to it by means of a paper clip was a sealed foolscap envelope addressed to me by hand.

Dear Sir ... then underlined ... *re: Estate of George Alan Lustre.* I read the convoluted legalese twice before its import fully penetrated my senses. I was being contacted *at the behest* of George Alan Lustre. Ploughing through the legalese, I was able to ascertain that Lustre had approached the Solicitors two years previously *(precisely)* to the date given on the *present letter.* Lustre had declared his intention of *absenting* himself from the UK for an indefinite period on *pressing business.* He then instructed that should the period of two years elapse without further contact from him, the Solicitors should proceed as follows:

i) In the first instance, a sealed envelope should be delivered to me.

ii) The Solicitors should hold possession of his properties and assets. In particular the full documented record of his researches held in a Safe deposit. (The relevant authorisation together with keys had been handed over).

iii) Before the formal reading of the Will, an updated version of which was kept in the Safe deposit, the complete record of his work should be placed with the Royal Society, along with copyright entitlement in the name of Lustre, for publication.

iv) The Will should be formally read in the presence of the named beneficiaries and the properties and assets disposed of as specified therein.

As one of the named beneficiaries, I would at a date, later to be notified, be requested to attend for the formal reading of the Will. I would be required to provide proof of identity. Currently there were matters of a legal nature being dealt with. It appeared that there were questions regarding as to whether Lustre's absence for the period of two years *constituted entitlement to the disposal of property and assets in Law.*

I opened the foolscap envelope.

My dear Foyle, you will by now know the circumstances connected with this letter. Since your visit, I forget how long ago that was, I have been completely immersed in work, leaving time or concern for nothing else. I believe I mentioned the need for Inducers of variable location, so as not to be tied to emissions to just one location, but to actually move the Inducers themselves at will. I rather think that I have arrived at a solution. I do believe the science to be sound, but of course, it needs to be tested with practicalities. My overall, perhaps fundamental, preoccupation has been and continues to be, the place of organic matter, in terms of its components within my field. In that respect, I have taken the work as far as I am able. It will be up to others to go further. All that I can now do and wish to do, is to validate my commitment to myself, if to no one else. To do so, it is sometimes necessary to involve that which is valuable and valued. I wish you to know that I have been glad of your friendship, even if at times it might not have appeared so. Much as I would have wished for the comfort of your presence, I could not in conscience place responsibility on you. I have instead opted for pre-set mode and copious details regarding procedure as well as precise co-ordinates for the location of the Inducer. Besides, had you been with me, I feared that your concern might have weakened my resolve to enter the Cube. Fare well in your endeavours. George.

I needed to sit down. I closed my eyes.

Fare you well also, old friend. Wherever you might be," I said. After a while. As to myself.

O Little Tower of Babel

In early morn, as is my wont, I walk the narrow path to open fields wherein, unleashed from restraint, my two faithful companions partake of exercise. It is summer. The lingering dew on the grass begins to leave at the gentle coaxing of the newling sun, leaving a freshness. It is a goodly time and circumstance for separation and quiet reflection.

Yester morn I walked in pensive mood with eyes downcast along the brambled path when one of my companions, given to voluble vocalising, gave urgent warning, in consequence of which I raised my gaze.

Advancing along the path, I beheld what impressed itself upon me as a haystack, albeit one of modest dimension. Prompted by the courtesy which marks my people, I withdrew into the encroaching overgrowth so as to concede right of passage. At proximity, I noted the supposed haystack to be proceeded by an elderly man garbed in workaday clothing, whose presence had been obscured from frontal view. He was wiry of build with a countenance of the hue and texture in semblance of walnut husk. The round dark lenses which shaded his eyes, together with the tight woollen hat pulled low, inclined his appearance toward the insectile. He walked with tentative step and body tilting backwards at alarming angle. As well he needed to, since his sparse frame served as counterbalance to the supposed haystack. For it he bore by means of a rake, held to the horizontal, with the handle at fulcrum point under one arm. He passed by me with ne'er a glance or word, absorbed in forced exhalation, stopping some five paces beyond me. He appeared to be gathering resolve and then with a heave and a sigh of grunted relief, he unburdened himself, of what I then took to be garden cuttings onto the bordering hedge.

I thought it prudent to permit return passage and was mildly surprised when the man stopped close to me. With some deliberation he rested the rake, downward pronged, on the ground, holding it with one hand at chest level. He then with equal deliberation brought his forearm to rest in limp manner on that which held the rake, in country fashion. He regarded me intently, or so I assumed, from behind the dark lenses for an interval touching on the disconcerting. After which he spoke thus:

"So. What sort of Art do you do then?" I must here give pause before venturing further. For the sake of intelligibility, I write his words in standard form. However, if I am to be faithful in the reporting, the phonetic import ran thus:

"Soow. Wha'so'ow Aaart doo ee doo then?" The abruptness and form of the utterance, together with the implications engaged my concern awhile.

"Pray, good sir," I made at length to enquire. "To what might you ascribe my practice of the Arts? Might it rest mayhap in that I sport a beard and my lower limbs are in corduroy clad?" My entreaty went unanswered. The man maintained his stance, which to a Victorian practitioner of the Arts might have given inspiration in depicting as 'The belligerent Enquirer'.

"'A've seen ee wi' stuff undery'r aaarm," further postulated the fellow with accusatory tenor to his tone, adding to my bewilderment. I searched in recollection as to what 'stuff', like his rake, might have been seen under my arm. I had indeed in times past involved in the practice of painting. But such tended to be the size of the canvases in general that to secure them underarm would have necessitated an extension of upper limb in excess of that of a Gibbon. I could only conclude that the fellow alluded to the mounting boards which on occasions I obtain from the purveyors of artists' materials. I utilise these to assemble collages of family photographs, an activity which periodically occupies me in the limp time of declining years.

"Well," I finally conceded. "I have in the past had involvement with painting and what might be perceived as sculpture." I spoke with due self-deprecating modesty which, I have on occasions been informed, is the invidious other face of arrogance.

"Aaah," exulted the fellow in the manner of one vindicated. "Soow then. Wha's aarder oyle or warrahcahlah?" Pursuing my line of alleged false modesty, I confessed to encountering extreme difficulty with both media, adding that the matter rested with the innate ability of the individual and the power of his vision.

"I'm good wi' warrahcahlah," the fellow admitted. "I did this warrahcahlah. Of St Michael's Mount it were. All they as saw i' wan'ed t'buy it. Them all reckoned it were better'an any fotigraaf." His demeanour briefly softened in satisfaction before reverting to his abruptness of persistent enquiry.

"Sooow. Wha' materials dooy'use in y'r sculpture then?"

"Mostly cardboard," I confessed.

"Caarbo'd?" he echoed in some distaste. "Ee caan't carve caarbo'd."

"I employ its use in layers," I explained in mitigation.

"Laayaars? Wha' so'o' caarbo'd is tha'?"

"Greyboard," I ventured.

"Nevver'erd of i'." I considered explanation in microns but decided otherwise. I searched for comparables.

"Do you remember the old-fashion shoe boxes? With shiny cardboard on the outside? Well inside it was grey and not shiny, wasn't it? That's the cardboard I used." I aimed for simplicity of explanation whilst wary of condescension.

"Bu' tha' be thin caardbo'd," the fellow surmised with incipient smirk. "Ee caan't doo nuthin' wi' thin caardbo'd like tha'." He then bent forward. "Ee caan't doo nuthin' bigger'an this." With that he indicated a space of some nine inches off the ground with the flat of one hand. "No bigger'an this," he repeated in some glee, which could have been interpreted as derision.

"Not always," I mused and then affecting a matter-of-fact tone, "I once had occasion to construct one piece … a tower … in excess of twelve feet in height." The information appeared to cloud the fellow's countenance. From the leaning posture, which he retained, he regarded me askance.

"Bu' thaa be taller'n y'self," he growled in affront.

"Most things tend to be so," I quipped, wishing to make merry. The fellow made to straighten, with some complaint from joints stiffened from overly held in single posture.

He uttered not another word nor looked in my direction. In its stead, he seized the rake as a bishop might his crosier or a penitent his staff and forthwith, the rake marking his pace, he progressed in truculent tread toward whence he came.

"It's been a pleasure to converse with you," I called out, true to the courtesy of my people, as ever. I tarried awhile, to follow in his wake at a distance of due discretion.

My Prostate Revisited

The word itself gives me trouble with the Rs. I never quite know if it's p(R)ostate, post(R)ate or p(R)ost(R)ate. One of those means 'lying down'. I know that much. But which? It's the English language. With it not coming naturally, I think I'm going along just fine with it and then I get tripped up in all sorts of little ways. It's so irregular. So many variations. So many exceptions. I pity the poor foreigners trying to get to grips with it.

As a case in point, my cousin Maury comes to mind. He spoke Spanish. At the time, he had been at daggers drawn with his dad. My aunt was at her wits' end and in desperation consulted the priest. Since my cousin Maury refused point blank to go to Confession, the priest advised a spell in the UK with me as the healthy option.

I met his flight and we stood outside the terminal waiting for the bus to take us into the City. Nearby, a newsvendor was busy shouting the odds in standard gibberish. I could see my cousin Maury straining to pick out the odd word. Defeated, he turned his attention to the propped-up news board with the headlines held with criss-crossed wire.

"Hhwot eet say?" he asked pointing to it. I read it out: "Festival Pronounced Success." My cousin Maury shook his head.

"Ey, Pepe," he said. "Dees Eengleesh lanhhuage eet ees harrd, noh?"

I tried to resolve my own difficulty with that elusive word using word association as an *aide memoire*. To avoid further complication, I looked for a similar word in Spanish. The nearest I could bring to mind was 'postre', meaning dessert or pudding. After some mental gymnastics to make the word fit for purpose, I gave up. It didn't work. At least not in the way I had hoped. I found, however, that during the time I was experiencing prostate issues, I developed a marked aversion to puddings of any sort, including tirfle … or is it trifle … which I had always supported avidly. In the end, I just settled for looking up the ominous word in my Collins Contemporary Dictionary prior to any medical appointment. You don't want to appear ignorant on top of being in agony and embarrassed to boot.

Then there was the location of the gland itself. I wasn't sure of that either to begin with. I was left in no doubt after the very first appointment, when I was told to lie on my side and latex gloves were snapped on.

I had similar issues with the diaphragm when I started singing lessons. Not having had occasion to concern myself with such matters, I held the vague notion of the diaphragm nestling behind the belly button and functioning as a sort of starter-motor, carburettor or distributor. Not that I was familiar with any of those things. I settled for the mechanical aspect after hearing the heart described as a pump. Apparently the diaphragm is more like a muscular corset. Mr Danvers-Gilchrist, my music teacher, was most disparaging on learning that, in my ignorance, I had been persistently breathing with my lungs, instead of from the diaphragm.

The prostate was a gland. That much I knew. As I also knew that glands swell when you have a cold or an infection. People feel between your jaw and your neck and tell you your glands are up. I suppose it wasn't altogether unreasonable to assume that there was a sort of gland centre around that area, with the prostrate somewhere in the vicinity of the neck. It wasn't all guesswork. I had some recollection of that being the case. It was only after encountering a certain derision, that I pursued the source of my knowledge. I found it in my Collins Contemporary Dictionary. *Prostate: a small gland at the neck … of the bladder …* well …

So. I get this pain which I haven't had before, although on occasions its nature has been used to describe my behaviour. At such times, my first port of call is my wife in her capacity as in-house physician. Once secure in the comfort of her concern, I can set about dismissing the pain as mere trirfle … trifle. It then involves a ritual of genetic gender reinforcement. I played it out admirably on the occasion of my hernia. Inguinal.

* * * * * * * * *

"I've had this nasty pain."

"Where … when … what have you been doing now?"

"Nothing. Well, other than breathing."

"I've warned you, haven't I? But no, you won't be told. I knew it would happen. I told you at the time."

"What time?"

"The time with the wardrobe."

"What wardrobe?"

"The one that got itself upstairs on its own."

"That was ages ago."

"So what could it be this time?"

"I dunno. I bent over to get this brush and I got this sharp pain."

"Pains don't come for no reason."

"Oh, stop fussing. It's nothing."

"You won't say it's nothing when you're writhing in agony from a strangulated or ruptured hernia."

"Alright. Alright. Next time I'll pick up a lighter brush. Dear oh dear. OK. OK. If it makes you happy, I'll make an appointment with the doctor. Anything for a bit of peace.

* * * * * * * * *

So. After numerous glove encounters of the familiar kind, I go in for a biopsy or cystoscopy, I forget which. Dr Karma takes me aside. It's an enlarged prostate. Advises prompt surgery. Wants to know if there's anything I'd like to ask. I daren't. Not with my grasp of anatomy. He lowers his voice. After the op. there may be a drop in the libido. In spite of myself, I wonder about its location. Dr Karma misinterprets my concern. He enlarges ... *sex*. Wants to know if I have any children. I'm on home ground. Barefoot and in a gown with a split back, I reclaim dignity. Seven lovely kids, I say. Dr Karma appears reassured. Says it needn't be a problem. He taps his temple: *sex starts up here*. There's me thinking it starts ... wrong again.

The pain became severe, as registering on the male scale. The reaction to it can be interesting. I suppose I must have been in a state of denial. I wasn't sure of Dr Karma's diagnosis. My self diagnosis inclined towards appendicitis, perhaps peritonitis. I was acquainted with the location of the appendix. I clearly remembered a school friend saying that the spot is exactly where your thumb is when you put your hand in your right trouser pocket. The discrepancy with Dr Karma's diagnosis I could attribute to 'referred pain'.

Another curious reaction showed up when the pain first kicked in. It may be that *in extremis* we revert to type or fall back on old thinking. Bent double, I blundered into the bedroom. I had actually opened the drawer where my underwear was kept, before it dawned on me what I was about to do. I would have laughed had I been able to. Instead I slammed the drawer shut.

In my formative years, it had been drilled into me to make sure to have on clean underwear when involved in an accident requiring hospitalisation. The use of the word 'when' rather than 'if' is significant. Not only does it imply the inevitability of a mishap, but it presupposes prior knowledge of it in order to ascertain the wearing of clean underwear. It further implies that the normal state of underwear is a matter of concern. Also, that the instruction is motivated by other than a regard for personal hygiene. At the time, suspecting that I had not been granted precognisance, I thought it was a bit much to expect me to change my Y-fronts every time I crossed a busy road. Just in case. Unguarded impulses are very revealing and, if typified by the example here given, best dealt with at professional level.

The day for the op. was fixed and I went in without undue qualms, bolstered by a fatalistic streak, accepting with good grace the inevitable, provided that in this case I was suitably zonked out. But that was before I saw Jack Pendrea and went out of my way to be kind. When I became traumatised in the short term with renewed anxieties some years later.

We were both admitted on the same day. He was an elderly man, although I was to learn that he was several years my junior. Perhaps he might have led a more interesting life than my own. He seemed to be in great distress although withdrawn. He did not involve in the usual introductions with other incumbents in the ward, but sat disconsolately on his bed at one end of the ward staring at the wall. He still sat, gently rocking back and forth after I had slipped into hospital garb, rationalised my bedside locker and paid the first uneventful visit to the toilets.

In a moment of aberration, I went over and introduced myself. He looked up as from a great distance, giving me the feeling of being invisible. Something seemed to stir within him causing rapid blinking. Aiming at joviality, I quipped:

"So, when are you booked for the slaughter?" Seeing mounting alarm in his eyes, I rephrased the enquiry.

"Have you been given a time for theatre?" This evinced a measured nod. Seizing the opportunity, I sallied forth engagingly.

"I'm booked for the matinée. Ten in the morning."

"After lunch. Jack Pendrea." I filled in the gaps made by the hollow voice.

"It's always a bit strange coming in for the first time," I ventured, judging his apprehension to lie along the unknown.

"Been here before. Never reckoned to be back," said Jack Pendrea, almost to himself.

"What are you in for?" I enquired with the available casualness.

"Hernia."

"Oh, hernia," I said brightly. "I've had that done. Nothing to worry about." He gave me a suspicious look. "No, you'll be up and about in no time. You'll feel so much better, you won't believe it." He shifted his position. His breathing altered.

"I've been worried, you see. You hear things, don't you? You say it's alright?"

"Absolutely. I'll give you a tip." The suspicious look returned. "When you come to after the op, you feel a bit sore that's all. Now, you probably feel you want to sort of hunch up in case you do some damage. Don't. Straighten up and the sooner the better, take a slow stroll along the covered way outside the ward. Once you've done that, you are on your way home. Don't go up or down any steps at first. When you do, take the weight on the leg opposite the side of the op."

"Oh, well. And you were alright after that?" asked Jack in lighter tone.

"Never looked back. Can't even see the scar."

"Oh, well. That's useful to know. Thanks. You hear all sorts, don't you?" Jack visibly relaxed and slipped effortlessly into anecdotal mode. He was Cornish born and bred; like all his family before him; his dad had been a miner; on his mother's side they were farmers; he was retired; worked for the Council; never been across the Tamar; knew this place when it was just fields. He appeared to notice me for the first time.

"What you in for then?"

"Prostate," said with nonchalance.

"Prostate?" Jack's face clouded over. "That's what I come in for last time. Never known pain like it in me life."

"You must have been grateful for the operation," I sympathised.

"Grateful?" Jack was affronted. "It were the operation that did it. Well that catheter thing anyway." I knew about the catheter. At first I had misunderstood the doctor when he explained about the catheter tube. I thought he said 'Cathode-ray tube', imagining it to be some form of advanced surgery.

"You need the catheter connected to the bladder to pass water after the op." I pointed out knowledgably.

"I know that," snapped Jack, somewhat accusingly I thought.

"It is inserted when you are under the anaesthetic," I continued instructively.

"I know that," repeated Jack quite aggressively. "It's not when they put it in. It's when they take it out. Never known pain like it. I couldn't take it. I had to tell the nurse to let me do it meself."

"Surely it couldn't have been that bad," I said to reassure myself.

"No" said Jack, oozing resentment. "Bad's not the word. Agony more like. Want to know what it felt like?" I didn't but he told me. "It was like they poked a rolled-up umbrella … you know, down there … and then they opened it and pulled it out." My knees snapped together like hydraulic clamps. Moisture impaired my vision.

That night of fitful slumber, furled black umbrellas, as starveling undertakers, stalked the ward. Sensing my fear they grouped in callous whisperings, then to approach and encircle my bed. They stood, ominous in their silence, necks craned in fixed intent. Watchful of the sleeper hunched in foetal dread. Watchful for the undulations in the sleep cycle. The time come, they began to move round. Slowly at first. Faster as the charged silence increased. Faster into a *dans macabre*. Now prodding. Now opening and closing like time-lapsed noxious toadstools. Advancing as I surfaced. Retreating as the depths claimed me.

* * * * * * * * *

I waded through a mixture of porridge and cotton wool towards consciousness. Arriving, I spent some time identifying my surroundings before groping for the thread of memory. I pulled at it getting as far as being taken on a trolley along a covered way and into a lift. Then along a dark corridor and into bright light and my left hand, between the wrist and the knuckles, being slapped quite hard. Then a blank. I retraced my thoughts to the trolley and after several attempts, managed to clear the gap and landed back in the ward. To the time of my introductory chat with fellow operatee and prophet of doom, Jack Pendrea.

At that moment, I was overwhelmed by a feeling which caused involuntary gathering of the legs, but which was abruptly cut short by a tugging sensation. Complete realisation flooded in, requiring a white-knuckle grip of the edge of my bed blanket.

There was no two ways about it. Sooner or later, I would have to take a look. I lifted the blanket. I was connected to a tube which extended beyond the bed. Viewed dispassionately, the arrangement was such as a plumber, with only access to tape and tubing, might effect as a temporary measure to divert a leak, while he fetched his tools.

O, fellow men. Such are we put on this Earth to endure. O, the barbaric width of that tubing. It challenged credulity. An affront to physiology, let alone masculinity: to nature itself, which doesn't design protuberances to act as receptacles. We are talking extreme gynaecology and obstetrics, fellow men. Of a kind denying the joy granted to our sisters in bringing forth new life. Ours an inverted birth.

Then began the countdown over the next three days, dread upon dread as the day of Jack Pendrea's prophesy drew near. At the appointed hour I followed Nurse Penrose, lamb-like and complete with attachment, into the Treatment Room. The oppressive central heating sprouted icicles along my spine. With virility at stake, I mounted the sacrificial couch. Nurse Penrose made ready. I put my affairs in order mentally at the same time entering a plea for mercy with some abstract entity, together with a bargaining resolution to mend my ways when, or if, I survived the ordeal.

"Try and relax," soothed Nurse Penrose. I nodded vigorously and clamped shut my eyes. The moment of truth arrived. The prophesy was fulfilled. The ordeal over. Tension erupted in overwhelming relief which clamoured for expression. I seized Nurse Penrose's hands and held them tightly. All I could think of to say was: *It's alright, Nurse. I'm not being funny.*

Nurse Penrose received a box of chocolates which matched the size of my relief. I returned home to resume life at full flow. With diligent self-debriefing, the association with the moonlighting activities of umbrellas was expunged. I revelled in the knowledge that at least I would not be going through the experience again.

Yeah, right.

* * * * * * * * *

Ten years later the errant gland once more claimed centre stage. With a vengeance. It brought a period fraught with complications, both clinical and administrative. There were deferred dates for the op.; cross-infections and an erroneous referral to an Orthopaedics Consultant which delayed the processing by a month.

Finally admitted, the spectre of the umbrella took its place along with other concerns, increasingly jumping the queue as time progressed.

One grey Thursday afternoon, I faced my Nemesis, met my Waterloo, crossed the Rubicon and entered Room 101: all in the space of one surreal half-hour.

Whereas in my previous jaunt I had been spared the experience of the catheter being inserted, safe in the merciful embrace of anaesthesia, this time round the procedure was to be performed while I retained token possession of my delirious senses. What was particularly galling in retrospect was to learn that the procedure had been unnecessary in the first place, the confusion arising from a mistake in patient identity.

A protracted swish of curtains isolated my bed from the ward. The swisher introduced herself as Dr Hamurabi. My unease at her gender and her youth, which appeared on a par with my younger granddaughters, flared to incandescence when informed by Dr Hamurabi that her mission was to catheterise me. In a torrent of barely coherent questioning, motivated by panic and compounded by five consecutive nights without sleep, I learned that Dr Hamurabi was Iranian; on her first month as interne and had not previously performed the intended procedure. To add spice to the occasion, her use of English was halting, adding a further dimension to mutual embarrassment, by her reliance on mime in communicating the more intimate instructions.

Being in a heightened state of closet delirium, I have no recollection of the number of abortive attempts at the procedure. I do know that at some point, Dr Hamurabi admitted defeat. Consulting her wristwatch, she gasped. As she hurriedly drew back the curtains, she said that she was late for the Consultant's afternoon ward round. With that, I was left exposed to the ward, in a state of incomplete attachment.

The period, however, was not entirely without its lighter moments. Following the Dr Hamurabi episode, the Top Man himself took control of the situation during his ward round. After pronouncements to his attentive team, none more so than a self-effacing Dr Hamurabi, regarding my condition, he instructed the Ward Sister to the effect that the traumatised patient be given a knock-out dose of something that night.

Come the morning, I woke to the welcome clatter of the tea trolley. Dressed to go off duty, the Night Sister came over to my bed. She appeared to be holding back a grin, which I took to be a sign of professional satisfaction at my obvious improvement after a good night's sleep.

Sister's professionalism slipped sufficiently for her grin to take over. I was to learn that my good night's sleep hadn't been entirely uninterrupted. It appeared that around three in the morning, I had been found wandering through the hospital corridors in great distress. When apprehended by the night staff, it seems I put up a spirited resistance, while lamenting that I was being thoughtlessly delayed. It appears that my anxiety centred on trying to find my wife, insisting that we had both been invited to a Jewish wedding in one of the local beaches and not only were we going to be late, but buses there were two-hourly.

Well, one reaches the point where one embarrassment more, or one less, is neither here or there.

Then there were the hallucinations.

It was necessary in the prevailing circumstances, to patronise the toilet facilities for periods of some length. On one occasion, at a loss for amusement, I found aesthetic value in admiring the simulated wood grain in the flooring. The way the grain by-passed the knots in the wood brought to mind the flow of water around boulders. Wishing to divert my attention from elsewhere, I continued to stare intently. As my concentration wavered, my vision became unfocused like happens in pensive state. It was then that it happened.

The wood grain appeared to lift from the wood. It began to swirl gently, then swooping into changing patterns as might a shoal of small fishes or clouds of roosting rooks. Going into a vortex, the pattern compressed into a tight ball. Startled, I refocused with a shake of the head. The ball imploded to pinpoint. The simulated wood grain on the flooring re-appeared.

The in-house entertainment picked up when I discovered that I could recreate the illusion at will. I was even able to bring variety to the programme on offer when, with a leap of intuition, I laid out an open newspaper on the floor. By turning over the pages, owing to the varying dispositions of print and images, wondrous three-dimensional images manifested. I was able to upgrade the programme when obliged to patronise the disabled facilities. There the flooring was one of small black and white tesserae. It may have been due to the marked contrast in the small tiles or perhaps their proliferation but, for whatever reason, two separate spheres arranged themselves: one glistening white; the other matt black. Actually, whatever the source materials, the configurations always presented in monochrome. But that was to change.

The upgrading into colour came at home. During the time I was discharged from hospital, allowing time for antibiotic treatment to take effect against an infection before being re-admitted for the actual operation.

I was in the kitchen, facing the doorway which gave into the hallway passage and the staircase to the upper floor, busy with some ironing, a task I have long taken upon myself in the family. I find it helpful as a means of separating out whilst allowing thoughts to wander. The front panels done, I lifted my good white cotton shirt over the ironing board and started on the back. For some reason, I looked up towards the doorway and froze.

Halfway up the stairway, which was in darkness with it facing away from light filtering through the glass in the front door, a golden sphere appeared suspended, gently rotating on varying axes. I would judge it to have been some twelve inches in diameter, seen from roughly twenty feet away.

I stood transfixed as it began to descend, passed through the doorway and came to rest an arm's distance in front of me at eye level. The random rotating of the sphere increased in speed. Swirling rings the colours of the spectrum intersected at the centre of the golden glow, which expanded to envelope me. I became aware of heat, rising in a haze, clouding the golden light. I backed slightly at the same time averting my eyes downward. With an urgent reflex action, I lifted my right hand, which held the iron away from the ironing board. There was no sign of the sphere. My good white cotton shirt bore the scorched branding of the Morphy-Richards' outfit.

Perhaps a differently disposed person might have seen mystical or spiritual implications in the apparition. For my part, I saw it as an enriching experience of the senses, marvelling at the combined power of chemicals and neurons to conjure up enchantment.

It is now coming up to six years since the second visitation from the mischievous gland, which came ten years after the previous one. It may be that I am ensnared in a ten-year recurring cycle. If so, I have four good years before I need concern myself with opening up my Collins Contemporary to ascertain where the R is placed in the P word, prior to the inevitable medical appointments.

The View from Below

I'm on the bus, right? Going home. Not that I'm broadcasting the fact to the world and his wife, like several of my fellow passengers with mobile phones velcroed to their ears.

There's this chap spread out on the seat in front of me. Clyde. Going by the tattoo surfing the double chin at the back of his shaven skull. He has already munched his way with obvious relish through a two-handed pasty, making sure to keep looking around contentedly so as to give everyone the chance to get occasional glimpse of his tonsils. He is now, with gassy enjoyment, slurping from a can of Kestrel. Clyde is obviously a man of action. 'JUST DO IT' urge the 9-inch yellow capitals on his black T-shirt. And he's got the combat trousers. Worn *à la mode*. From the overhand of his bum. He had some difficulty negotiating the aisle to his seat. On account of having to walk with a slouching sprawl of his legs, so as to prevent the trousers from falling down. He's got the spanking new expensive trainers. Naturally. There are other tattoos to go with the identity one. Maori tribal patterns. On both arms. Like threadbare sleeves. Also oozing on his neck from under the T-shirt. And one other one. Summarising Clyde's emotional range: *LOVE* and *HATE*. Writ on the knuckles. Then there are the piercings. One on the outer edge of the left eyebrow. Five on the right ear. One on the lobe. Four on cartilage.

Nah, Steve … gone past B&Q (silly Steve) … getting up to Tesco now … s'right (Steve's in the picture) *… Nah Steve … not that Tesco* (as you were) *… not the Big Tesco going up the hill … s'right … the other by the roundabout* (Steve's got it) *… seen Malc yet? … nah me neither … yep … yep … the other bloke got it worse though … yeah … yeah … wicked …nah, that's tomorrow night … yep … yep … me too … be a laugh … yeah alright … seela'er … take care.* All that technology. All that bouncing off satellites. Time for a musical interlude now. In go his earplugs. Here we go. *Tssh tssh tssh.* On and on. Seeping from the plugs. Like an argumentative mosquito with a lisp.

Normally my eyeballs would be rotating anti-clockwise, starting at 6 o'clock. But not today. Not today, Joseph. Not even with the rain hammering against the windows of the bus. Another seasonal deluge. The wettest July since the Mesozoic apparently. No. All is serenity. The bus' windscreen wipers, usually a source of squeaky metronomed irritation, dance to a sinuous improvised *pas de deux*. God is in His Heaven and all's well with His creation. I feel well disposed towards the entire universe and all its denizens. One such in particular.

Moi.

There is good justifiable reason for my expansive state. Behind the serenity lies the satisfaction from no mean achievement. Wrenched in the face of serious personal handicaps. The main of these can be attributed to simply being of the male gender, compounded by a nature given to abstraction of thought. Certainly not ideal qualities for, what is termed in magazine culture, 'multi-tasking': an ability visited on the female to perform several tasks simultaneously. Whilst also talking. In contrast, the male lumbers from thought to thought; from single task to single task. A kind of tunnel existence. Some, of less than generous disposition, might want to deprive me of my satisfaction by pointing out that the tasks which constituted my achievement were performed sequentially and therefore lacking the element of simultaneity ascribed to the female. This I would refute by insisting that the tasks being performed sequentially was due to the generally accepted view that logic is largely visited on the male, which would require the tasks to be performed in a certain order and with single focus. It in no way precludes the ability to consider and weigh the tasks simultaneously.

I woke with a feeling of optimism, which invariably gets moderated as the day begins its demands. But today the feeling was to persist and here I am returning home with an appreciable number of Brownie points, despite the inherent deficiencies mentioned and the hour approaching lunchtime.

The feel-good factor had one significant reinforcement. In referring to it, I have no wish to be indelicate, but neither should I be circumspect and in being so, fail to give credit where it's due.

At a certain time of life, with its attendant complications, few signs better portent the coming of a good day than a satisfactory bowel movement.

As a form of augury, with tea now encased in bags, for sheer reliability it is preferable to studying the entrails of pigeons. Because of their nature and in the interests of propriety, it is all too easy to overlook the importance of base functions in determining one's general outlook on life. That final consummation of the elusive sneeze; the surrender to the recalcitrant yawn; the liberating of twisted intestines in the release of flatulence; not to mention eleventh hour access to a loo in dire need, all bring solace touching on the spiritual. With them comes a pleasure of a different order of magnitude to that derived from the contemplation of beauty, Art or Music as well as that from intellectual pursuits. For the latter, unlike the former which is of natural design and therefore brings the reassurance of well-being and is accessible to all, needs to be cultivated and varies with individuals and societies. When it comes to the crunch, physiology leaves metaphysics at the starting line.

Discomfort and pain can similarly intrude on philosophy. And when it comes to the relief from severe pain, we float with the Angels.

In the 70's, against my better inclination, I was roped in to accompany a colleague on a Geography School trip to Edale in the Peak District. My knowledge of the subject was nil and my interest negligible. Apart from general herding, my brief was to deliver a photographic record of the trip including aspects of the study involved.

No sooner were we billeted in the wilds than I was visited by severe pain involving a chasm in a back molar. I have no idea how during that week I managed to conceal the agony, not wishing to disrupt the work schedule, to go in search of rural dentists. Somehow I clicked away along the mountain paths, ravines and down disused mines. By the end of the week I came to appreciate the splendour of Mam Tor as a suicide venue. The journey home I cannot describe. All I remember is staggering indoors in near collapse, my wife grabbing her coat there and then whilst giving hurried instructions to our children.

I have no recollection of the Southend/London Express coach or of getting to Guy's Hospital, where my wife knew from her nursing days they operated an emergency Dental Clinic dealing mainly with road accidents. I do remember my Angel of Mercy remonstrating with Reception when being told that the Duty Surgeon was in Theatre. I remember the stomp through hollow corridors and my wife standing four-square outside double doors labelled Theatre. After an eternity the doors opened and out came a figure in green costume. In a blur my wife accosted the figure; I was propelled into a room; an instant of crunching excruciation and then the Heavenly Host stood revealed in all its glory.

The streets of Paddington were suffused in golden light. Motley brick glowed with the blush of Carrara marble at sunset. The celestial tinkling from the Music of the Spheres was all around. I wanted to hug my fellow-man. As it happened the streets were deserted. I flew home on downy wings. High above the dismal sodium glower: ahead of me, stretching beyond horizons, God's creation in verdant freshness.

My wife had the good grace to withhold telling me until a later date, that my religious ecstasy was due to the cocaine used in the anaesthetic for the extraction. That in itself poses interesting questions, which I best not dwell on for the present, having already strayed somewhat from the progress and theme of my bus journey.

Well, to continue. I was up early, washed and breakfasted, in expectation of the engineer from South West Water calling. I had reported a drastic drop in water pressure and not being given a time for the visit, I was reconciled in the spirit of my optimism, to put the day on hold from 8am to 8pm. However, true to the favourable augury for the day, he called at 9am on the dot.

With the further reinforcement of the feel-good-factor, I led the way into the kitchen where the engineer experienced at first hand the miserable performance of the mixer tap. After appropriate sucking-in of breath, indicating the severity of the problem, he was able to satisfy himself about there being no ongoing roadworks in the vicinity which could account for the geriatric dribble giving the lie to the rampart arrogance of the chromed spout. After a period of reflection, he concluded that the problem might be centred on the pressure unit of the tap. This had followed my timid suggestion that since the pressure upstairs was OK, it might be so. *We get a lot of that.* Now, I will here confess to sensing the first cracks appearing in the optimism of the day. I was aware, from past experience, of the tendency in manufacture to make parts interdependent. I was well on the road to visions of the pressure unit needing a new tap which went with the sink unit which went with the other units, ending with a new fitted kitchen. And that before call-out fee and labour from a plumber.

I'm OK with anything to do with wood, but show me metal or plastic and I'm lost. It's a mental block. Like my aversion to cucumbers (I don't take kindly to the Freudian suggestions of deep-seated 'penis envy'. I am satisfied of the origin being dietary). However, rather than shell out for a new kitchen, I resolved to confront the phobia and tackle the problem hands-on.

"Do you think you could undo the tap, sort of, and show me what the pressure unit looks like?" I ventured.

"Do you have an adjustable spanner?" asked the engineer. I seized the moment and hastily repaired to my garage, where I keep an adjustable spanner thing just to appease the Gods.

"This is it," said the engineer after asking to borrow a screwdriver. "You can get one in B&Q." I studied the part intently, struggling to impress its shape and place within the tap and my reluctance.

"Would you mind assembling the tap. We best not be without some water. I'll get myself to B&Q this morning," I further imposed.

"There we are," said the engineer, returning the tools. Wishing to impress him, or perhaps myself, with my competence for the job in hand, I turned on the tap. Lo and behold, the water came on at full pressure.

"We get a lot of that," explained the engineer. "Sometimes people turn off the tap too hard and the rubber washer gets compressed." Phew. No need for a new kitchen. The augury holding true.

So. Off to catch the bus to Redruth. The No.18 draws up just as I get to the stop, wouldn't you know it. First task, with due regard for the priority and locations of the numerous undertakings envisaged. Nationwide Building Society. *Update the book then transfer £200 from the ISA to the Flex. Not the other way round or you'll land us in overdraft.* Tick. Clinton Cards. *Something suitable for a two-year old birthday. A boy. Use your judgement. Also for an eighteen-year old. Girl. Something a bit special. Doesn't have to have 18. Might as well get a few for general use as well.* Tick. Wilkinsons. *When are you going to do something about the kitchen light? If you can't do it, let's get an electrician in.* The starter motor. It's got to be that. Must make sure to get one conforming to British Standards. The one in place I bought from the Pound Shop. Made in China. Promptly went on the blink, turning the fluorescent tube into strobe light. Shoe repairers. Collect the tan pair with welted soles. *Next time don't leave it so late so you need complete new heels.* Tick. Arts and Graphics. Uniball pens. Fine. Black/blue/red/green. Useful to use different colours for successive drafts when writing. Avoids mix-ups. Tick. Library. Return 'The God Delusion'. Only two days overdue. *It's silly to have to pay fines. All you have to do is pick up the phone and renew it.* Tick. 'Good Impressions'. E-mail with attachments and Final Proof Approval for 'Second Coming and Other Upheavals' to Authorhouse. Tick. Collect typed stories for 'The view from below and other Peerings'. Tick. Vacuum repair shop for Dyson belt. (£1.02). Dysons wanted £12 for same plus call-out fee for engineer. Not covered by Comprehensive Guarantee. Tick. Knitting Shop. 1½ metres elastic. *No wider than 2 cms. It's for a skirt waistband. Not a Roman Siege catapult.* Tick. Collect my repeat prescription for Fluoxetine capsules. *You don't want to run out of those.* Tick.

By any standard of pedantry and trumpet-blowing a commendable achievement for one of the genus Mono-Tasker, with some justification for self congratulation. Moreover, accomplished with good grace and with the optimism streak intact. All the more remarkable when, given the likelihood of … hello … fellow-me-lad has pressed the bell. But not before bringing Steve up to speed and taking out a thin roll-up from a tin. Two elderly shoppers are fumbling with their four-wheel trollies. Our Clyde steals the march on them, as they struggle to get them into gear, with a precipitated waddle down the aisle. *Cheers mate* to the driver. As soon as he alights Clyde is turning his body this way and that to get the better of the driving rain, desperate to light up. The driver looks on impassively, wrists on the steering wheel, as the elderly shoppers begin the slow, perilous descent. The doors bang shut and we're off again.

Someone is pumping the bus to a stop at the next 'request'. The doors yank open. A boot appears on the platform. Mid-calf length. Splayed open by the absence of laces. It's seen better days but the rain, like snow on a junkyard, has worked its magic.

"Do you go to St Ives?" calls a girl from without. She's quite young despite her appearance. Drenched to the skin. Fits the category of 'traveller' or 'New Age'. Possibly residual 'hippie'. Cerise dreadlocks, green mascara, generous piercings, abundant beads and bracelets, denim jacket, long flowered skirt.

"No, love. You want the number 14," replies the driver in weary standard impersonal.

"Awesome," intones the girl flatly, without the merest hint of the slightest concession to irony.

Awesome.

Awesome?

AWESOME? … You are drenched to the skin from standing God knows how long in a downpour waiting for a bus which may come, if at all, the Holy Ghost knows when and It's not telling … and that fills you with awe? The bus doors slam shut with incredulity.

That's it. My serenity. My equanimity. Hanging by a thread at the best of times, straight out the window. Had the girl said something on the lines of 'bloody fucking buses', I'd be OK and continue contentedly to journey's end. For if we disregard the unnecessary overload in the use of both adjective and adverb to describe buses, it would nonetheless accurately reflect the exasperation of the situation. Instead we get *awesome:* a vacuous umbrella expression, hatched in the hothouse of American upbeat 30+ sitcoms, covering anything from the topping of a pizza to the Grand Canyon.

Of course I'm getting hot under the collar. We are talking 'serious' here. This is corruption. Insidious. From within. The stuff that topples empires. It's what happens when we lose touch with reality; with a sense of the appropriate. When desensitised to value judgement we drift along with whatever influences in thought, response and behaviour are prevalent. I may need to vent further concern in this regard, as has been shown by this Summer of Sport. But for the moment concern must remain with the girl. As it needs to for this is no trivial situation being overblown. It might appear so. But it carries the vestiges of the missing nail from the horse's shoe accumulating in the battle being lost or the ship going down for want of a dab of tar. It's the rash that surfaces as symptom of a deeper malaise.

What adjectival Everest would the poor soul confront if presented with something truly momentous. Truly awe-inspiring: say a personal apparition from the Virgin Mary; or a win on the quadruple rollover of the Euro lottery as the result of the winning numbers being prophesied in a dream. How might she describe her feelings to the battery of microphones? I venture to suggest that it might be something on the lines of *cool* or *an OK experience.*

To a lesser or greater degree and for a variety of reasons, we all default on the appropriate. We drag ourselves to the doctor feeling like something the cat sicked up. What doesn't hurt itches. Forehead steaming. Hair made of string. Spine like crushed ice. Joints super-glued. Finger nails electrified. We go into the consulting room.

"Hello, how are you?" says the doctor, who should know better than to ask. What do we say? … *well since you ask* … and forthwith embark on a histology of our ailments, real and imagined, beginning with A and worthy of the Complete Family Health Encyclopaedia? … well no.

"Fine thanks," we manage to chirp. At least in the case of the dentist and hygienist, we are spared. As they rattle off anecdotes, firing intermittent questions, we are not obliged to say anything we might later regret. With a mouth full of powered implements, we can get away with utterances on the lines of a ventriloquist's *goggleogeer*, such as gah geh geeh go goo, or combinations of these, relying on intonation to convey assent, denial, mild surprise or incredulity.

Stopping again. What's this? A contingent of four-wheelers pressing forward with elbows at the ready. It's the rain. Brings them out in droves. Might be another Deluge. Best be on the safe side and stock up with supplies. Might be an idea to pick up a live dove from Pets-R-Us. Well you never know. *Please allow passengers to get off before boarding.* The driver's resting his wrists on the steering wheel again, eyelids and mouth in severe droop. Could do with traffic lights inside the bus. Standing room only now. *Please move on towards the back.* Hang on. General disruption. A buggy coming aboard. A two-tier job with ballast of multiple plastic bags. A reshuffle of seats and trollies. Disadvantaged by the courtesy gene, I give up my seat, glowering daggers at several unlovely youths with dancing thumbs, plugged ears, heads bowed in concentration. A delay. What's up? A shopper can't find her Bus Pass. Always one. Has been standing outside waiting for the best part of a week but hasn't thought to get the Pass ready.

It's in my purse … must be in this bag … no … funny … can't say it is … can't be in this one … I put the fish in there … must be this one … ha ha … right at the bottom … A fumble through the purse's filing system … *no … funny … I usually keep it next to the loyalty cards … Ah … hang on.* The driver looks pointedly at his watch … *Ah … got it … I always like to keep it handy.* Out comes the Pass. From the cardigan pocket. Inside the coat. Just one more to go. A man. Tugging at something. In lollop two obese dogs. Some discussion regarding tariff for multiple four-legged passengers. The man's not convinced. Hands over a £20 note reluctantly. An imperceptible *Tsk* from the cashier. Oh well, we've got the smell of damp dog to add to the general fug with windows shut and heating at full blast. The doors shut with a bad-tempered judder. On go the wipers, screeching away for all they're worth.

Oh hello. Running ahead of the bus. Silly sod. A fitness freak. It gets the unlovely youths banging on the windows making Zoo noises. One, outdoing his fellows, goes into mime. Pumping one hand up and down with fingers curled. We overtake and pass the runner with the youths' involvement reaching crescendo. They are all into mime now. Index and middle fingers in upward jerks.

The runner's not in the first flush. Old enough to know better. Obviously prey to the seasonal bug *Olympicus Britanicus* or the recurring *Marathonis Londinium*. On he plods, splashing away, his face dripping noble intent. He's got all the gear of course, except for an umbrella: aerodynamic running kit; advanced trainers; designer shades; stop-watch; headband; earplugs and bottled water in defiance of the free-ranging abundance.

Dear oh dear. I'm trying to get over the distress at the girl's difficulties and now this. Another reminder of this tendency to hook on to whatever trend is prevalent. Don't get me wrong. I've nothing against running in itself. We've been given legs and there are occasions when we need to 'leg it'. Fast. No. This again is something else. Another example of the skin rash alerting to systemic malfunction.

In fairness the condition largely manifests in the current age group between the ages of 20-40. But there is alarming evidence of older groups being infected. As yet there is no substantial evidence of my age group being affected. There are isolated cases but these can be discounted on grounds of emotional immaturity, learning difficulties, alcohol or confirmed bachelorhood. In this regard we who qualify as fathers, grandfathers and great-grandfathers, can withdraw gracefully to the sidelines, from there with the smugness of accumulated wisdom, to pontificate in general disapproval.

It's as if in our more active years we are subject to indeterminate influences or pressures which, like the rumble of the elephant and the chittering of the insect, lie outside our band of conscious registration. So we go this way and that guided or in response to the ultra/sub sonic signals. For all we know it may be part of a cunning plan by Nature to keep the species stimulated and away from stagnation. If so, we can be sure that there will be total indifference and disregard for any notions which we might hold regarding progress, aesthetics or morality. A case of change for change's sake.

We are going along swimmingly and along comes a shift. Small to start with, involving a tiny minority setting out their store of individuality. If the stirring gathers momentum it can attain critical mass and become the benchmark for aspiration. Inevitably what starts as rebellion to conformity then becomes conformity, complete with uniform. In that respect, Clyde's shaven skull and combat trousers are no different from my beard and cords. If there is a difference, it may lie in that Clyde may find sweetness in being part of something while I savour the tart taste in the feeling of not running with the herd.

We can, with varying degrees of resistance, absorb considerable changes in comparatively short periods of time, going from, say, the bloomer to the thong, the crinoline to the skirt on its way to being a belt. Then there's the sensitive area of men's hair. There are still occasional sightings of 'short back and sides with side parting' but these are rare and have survived the onslaught of the crew cut, Jesus locks, perms, Afros, ponytails, Mohicans and the prevalent shaven skulls. This latest is a veritable boom for the prematurely bald or, should I say, follicley-challenged. It delivers a 'hard man' look which can be considerably enhanced with compensatory designer stubble and, going the whole hog, with tribal tattoos and wearing a pair of those bizarre long shorts or short longs with the low-slung bulging pockets.

I fear that changes are afoot though, if young males in the Soaps and footballers are anything to go by. It could well signal a schism between the established shaven skulls, anxious to retain entrenched values, and the adherents of what I would term the New Blockhead style. It could well be a sign of the times since similar divisions threaten the unity of the Established Church on the fundamental question of whether or not the distaff side has the genetic entitlement, preferably reinforced by Scriptural sanction, to hold a Bishop's Crosier. We live in troubled times.

I find the New Blockhead personally unsettling. It brings to mind the drawings of Georg Grosz depicting a type of brutal reveller in Pre-War Germany. The look can also be evident in the intimidating, stiff-necked U.S. Marines on Presidential escort ceremonial. Where the New Blockhead differs from the military variety is in that in addition to the short back and sides, it boasts a ruffled bouffant top, effectively increasing the ascent of the neck, typical of the look. Perhaps 'Retro-Basin' might be a more apt description of the style, since it might echo in intent the tendency to the homespun or pseudo-shabby evident in the practice of tearing the knees of expensive jeans.

(Whatever would one do if sarcasm hasn't been invented? Languish in incoherence I shouldn't wonder.)

Irrespective of what covert influences might determine trends or changes, we cannot disregard those of television, magazines, newspapers and novels. Of these it can be assumed that television carries the highest likelihood, if only by the fact that it is ensconced in practically every home. Certainly we can aim at being discriminating and be selective in viewing. But even then we are exposed to 'seepage' in the form of presentation and the relative importance given to topics of the day. Even if restricting ourselves to just and only the News, it cannot be avoided. Once we could rely on the News for sobriety. Not any more. Not since one lady Newsreader or other shoved aside the newsdesk to prove that the species had legs and, standing on them, advanced in a split skirt with Dancing School mannered steps. Then, of course we have the … oops … another runner being overtaken.

It's getting to be an epidemic. This one's old enough to have forgotten his Bus Pass … dear oh dear. The knees look as if they don't belong to him. Still, he's game. Let's hope he hasn't got grandchildren. Animated response from the unlovely youths. Guffaws. Bent backs with simulated walking with stick's the preferred mime … oh, hang on. There's more. A couple this time. This is reaching pandemic. Get the gear. Matching tracksuits. His and hers. Pink … give me strength. The unlovely youths gawp, strangely quiet.

All this get-out-and-go. Well, I suppose it's to be expected. It has, after all been a Glorious Summer of Sport: Olympics; Para-Olympics; Tour de France; various Marathons; Wimbledon; Formula One; Cricket; Golf; Snooker; Darts; Club Bowls. The entire Nation caught in an upsurge of National identity and pride. A time to rejoice. To celebrate commitment, selfless endeavour, goodwill, fair play and physical prowess. To bask in the glow from the power of Sport to unite peoples in peace and harmony and to inspire future generations. Or so the media, TV in particular, would have us believe.

* * * * * * * * *

Now. We need to have consensus on this. Across the board. None of this British stiff-upper lip, gallant loser rubbish. We are up against Johnny Foreigner and he's not backward in coming forward. We want medals. Plenty of medals. Medals of all colours. We want to be up there on the table, snapping at the heels of the Chinese with all their unfair advantages. Enough medals to stop the Moaning Minnies bleating on about the billions being better spent on schools, hospitals, pensions, jobs blah blah blah. At all times coverage must be positive and up-beat. Avoid mention of the Dome. Stress the benefits of regeneration and legacy for the young which, of course, go beyond mere economics. We want 'fantastic', 'incredible', 'amazing', 'astounding'. Do mention the sterling work of the thousands of volunteers. We all have a little of the Traffic Warden in us. Give us a role, preferably with some sort of uniform and we're happy. It will be 'an experience of a lifetime', a warm recollection of 'I was there'. Little enough for the saving in wages. While on wages, there's been an unexpected bonus. A last-minute default from the Security Contractors X^{10}-4^2. A triple whammy. Millions saved in wages with our boys and girls in khaki jumping into the breach. Beats Afghanistan. With the M.O.D. picking up the tab. Then after the Games, compensation for breach of contract. Win win win. One final word. Spectators. Plenty of shots of them. Let them see themselves on the big screen. Does wonders for excitement. Plenty of 'hello Mum' shots, Mexican waves and 'look at me with my face painted red white and blue. Outrageous or what'. Oh, any empty seats in the less popular events. Fill them with our boys and girls in khaki.

* * * * * * * * *

Cynical? I don't think so. Can't claim to be a realist in response because reality is subjective and liable to be built on shifting sands. No. Before I am rendered incapable by the howls of outrage, we might remind ourselves of one fact. Namely that the worship of supreme physical attainment in the temples and arenas of sport is underpinned by Fast Food and Fizzy Drinks conglomerates. It's a fact of life. Just as the highest accolade for contribution to World Peace rides on the back of

High Explosives. We live with contradictions. The importance we give to sport as necessary for the development of youngsters doesn't quite square up with the selling off of school playing fields to make room for congestions of luxury flats.

It's not a question of the facts in themselves but rather of our awareness and acceptance of them. A case of calling a spade by the name on the Birth Certificate. Somewhere between the extremes of 'summink yer dig wiv' and 'a metallic implement of spatulate configuration with extended handle, employing the principles of the Fulcrum and Cantilever for the displacement of soil'. In so doing we can better maintain a sense of relative values and more of a sense for the appropriate.

* * * * * * * * *

Here is the News. The main item. Another glorious day for Team GB with yet another gold and a remarkable bronze in front of an ecstatic capacity crowd. The gold sets a new world record. A full $\frac{1}{200}$th of a second off the previous record held since the first Games by Tiredisis. The bronze represents an amazing achievement topping an all-time personal best. Bill Hyperbole who was present at this incredible day of amazing achievement for British Sport, has the details. Over to you Bill. Thank you. Yes, Eunice, as you say an unbelievable afternoon with Team GB rampaging through the Medal Table. I have here with me the British-born Banatusi Forenbodi. Banatusi, a remarkable achievement. A full $\frac{1}{200}$th off the record held since the first Games. In front of your home crowd as well. You must be over the moon. Yes, thank you Bill. It's incredible, unbelievable, I can't believe it. I've been training for this 48 hours a day from the day I was born and dreaming about it from before then. Hard work. But at the end of the day, I went out there and did the business. I've got to thank everyone who has supported me in my victory. First there's … Banatusi, what about the crowd? … yes marvellous, incredible, unbelievable … first there's my trainer who believed in me and when … Banatusi, sorry to interrupt you … the crowd wants you for the lap of honour draped with the British Flag … now we want to bring Harry Harrier to the microphone to tell us about his unbelievable achievement in topping his personal best. We'll do so just as soon as he's off the recovery position. In the meantime here's Percival Updike … Percival, you've won a total of 26 golds over the last ten Olympiads. You know what it takes … Yes Bill. You've got to go out there and give it your best. Thank you Percival. Harry's not quite ready, so for the moment, back to you Eunice. Thank you Bill … here's the rest of the News … 1,000 feared dead and ½ million made homeless as the flood in A sweeps everything in its path … the famine in B reaches humanitarian crisis as refugees pour into neighbouring C … despite talks with the ruling party, Special Envoy Tee Annon's 66-point peace plan collapses, with the greatest casualties on both sides reported to date and the region plunged into Civil War … and now here is the main story again … Another glorious day for Team GB … Music from the film 'Chariots of Fire' … voice-over announcement … There will be full coverage of today's events with the achievements of Team GB in an extended programme replacing Newsnight tomorrow night. You will also be able to see full coverage together with extended interviews on Sunday in place of Sunday Life, to be followed with live coverage of the Machu-Picchu Formula 1 Grand Prix.

The recovering Harry Harrier's achievement would have been of an even greater order of magnitude during the Bronze Age Olympics, with silver and gold not being in circulation.

* * * * * * * * *

Another glorious day for Team GB with Hurrragh Huggunk triumphing over the visiting tribes to firmly put his tribe in contention for top honours. The British-born Hurrragh had the capacity crowd off their haunches throughout the 100 paces race. The grunting was deafening, spurring the local man to superhuman effort. For 4 full hours the runners bunched and jostled as they delayed crossing the finishing line. It was then that the 48 hours-a-day training of Hurragh paid off. In a masterly manoeuvre, he put on a spurt as if intending to cross the finishing line. The field followed suit. Hurrragh came to an abrupt stop, wrong-footing the field. In the confusion he pulled off the tactical master stroke. With shoulder charges in quick succession, he sent two of the runners over the line into first and second position, dashing over himself to claim third place and bronze glory.

* * * * * * * * *

Oh good. The fat dogs are getting off. Perhaps we'll be able to breathe a little more easily. One doesn't want to go out in the rain. Has to be dragged, claws scraping. Where was I? … Oh yes. On about Sport and Sponsorship from Fast Food people and the like. It's not that I have any beef against Burgers-R-Us at the personal level. I quite enjoy a burger occasionally, provided it's easy on the veg. When I had exhibitions, I used to take our grandchildren around in their various family groups. I always made it a point to end up at Burger Emperor afterwards, so as to avoid cultural overload. Now they lecture me on healthy lifestyles, organic products and renewable energy. It seems that a fifth rider has joined the Apocalypse Four, bringing 'Obesity'. As to be expected, he has difficulty keeping up with the gallop, but he is gaining ground.

For my 75th birthday my wife took me to Burger Emperor and then to see the film 'Chicago'. I love musicals … no … nothing like that. In particular those like 42nd Street, Chorus Line and Cabaret. It's the tight verve of the dance routines. It's the American musicals. I can't speak for the home-grown. I once saw Salad Days … dear oh dear. I'm OK with Oklahoma, Carousel, The King and I and the like. South Pacific is the fly in the ointment. In the film they had to cart in an Italian actor to play, adding insult to injury, a Frenchman in the romantic lead. Couldn't sing, couldn't dance, couldn't speak American. Only *Cherie* this and that and all that *come with me to the Casbah* stuff. Then to put the top hat on it, there was that unforgettable Christmas Show when every known male TV presenter donned Yankee Sailor uniform and gave us 'There is nothing like a dame', complete with fake gymnastics … oops, there goes another runner, revelling in the rain. Each to his own.

Nothing wrong with sport for harnessing the exuberance of youth. Or indeed for keeping fit generally. It's particularly important these days for the young, following the scarcity of school playing fields, and their tendency to limit their exercise to their thumbs.

The problems start when sport gets serious and it's a case of winning at all costs to the exclusion of all else. In this regard, there runs a pernicious streak through professional sport. When it's winning by fair or foul means. In addition to ongoing pressure to excel, there are inducements in the form of exorbitant recompense in prizes and product promotion.

It's another of the sad facts of life that the advertisers, those dedicated manipulators of choice, have so little regard for 'the punters'' intelligence and susceptibility. It has long been a rule of thumb that a scantily-clad model is essential for product promotion. The swing is now towards celebrities, among which are numbered outstanding sportspersons. Anyone excelling in pedalling, running, jumping high or far, able to place a small ball with a minimum of shots into a small hole, or a maximum number of times a larger ball into a large net or indeed propel any size ball effectively – such a person is well placed to influence our choice of cereal or hair product.

* * * * * * * * *

OK. Listen up, guys. Today we are going to deal with the nitty-gritty. OK, so you've trained 48 hours a day since birth and dreamed of glory before then. At the end of the day, you've gone out there and given it your best. The crowd has been amazing. You've got your medal. The offers of product promotion are coming in. You've got to be in peak condition. The competition is fierce. Now then. On the table is a range of products with the highest rating in terms of financial return. Right. Each of you in turn is going to select a product. OK? Right. Who's going to start the ball rolling? Anyone? Yes. Adrian. Now I want you to look straight into the camera. Speak clearly. In your own words now, how would you convince the viewer about the excellence of the product ... go. 'Yeah. I've trained 48 hours a day since I was born. It's been my dream of glory before then. So at the end of the day, I went out there and did the business. The crowd was amazing. I get out every morning before it's light and give it a hundred per cent. Yeah ... and oh ... every time I have a bowl of ... er ... Action Flakes.' Yes. Very good Adrian. You covered all the main points. Not quite in the right order. The sincerity came across. We may need to do some work on the voice. In terms of emphasis mainly. Right. Who's next. Great. Off you go .... 'I like to feel good and look great. So every morning, after I get up when it's still dark, I use my Robinson 5-blade pivotal self-adjusting safety razor with X-06 intrinsic lubricant. My face feels smooth and fresh. It gives me the confidence to start on my daily 48 hour ...' Thank you. That's great. To the point. Succinct. Perhaps, though, we should let one of the chaps deal with that particular product, Cynthia.

* * * * * * * * *

Please. Just take the money and run. On second thoughts, don't run. Not for a while. Have the money wired to your off-shore account ... hmm rain seems to be easing up. No more sign of the four-wheelers. The wipers still going for old times' sake.

One off-spin of this Summer of Sport has been the upsurge of interest and support for the Para-Olympics. A very positive move against discrimination. I find myself, at times however, caught in the quandary of positive discrimination through not knowing how to refer to the athletes without giving offence: is it 'ability-impaired' or 'ability-challenged' or 'proportionally-able'? I know it's not 'disabled', although I would imagine it would be advisable to use the term when claiming Disability Benefit Allowance. I know for a fact it is not 'handicapped'.

* * * * * * * * *

The Club President has asked me to put the word about that his nephew is going to be joining. Apparently awfully keen on golf. Seems he has some condition. So, a word to the wise. When discussing your game on the green or in the clubhouse, best to steer clear of mentioning your handicap. We don't want the gutter press getting hold of the wrong end of the stick and kicking up a hoo-ha.

* * * * * * * * *

There is also the vexed question of assessing the relative level of ability of the athletes in the interests of fair competition. In addition to individual ability there has to be consideration given to the hardware employed in certain events. There was an instance of heated dispute during the Games when a competitor claimed the winner of the event to have had unfair advantage in the extra length of the running blades. It raises questions regarding the need for rigorous scrutiny and regulation of the design and tensile qualities of the hardware involved. As things stand the Governing Bodies are stretched enough in the vigilance for performance enhancing substances in fully-able competition, not that at … oh.

The rain has stopped. The wipers have gone into remission. Looking through the windscreen, I note that from on high a pale wash of cerulean makes shy request for admission to the day … as you were … I'm looking through a tinted band on the glass.

This thing about commercial sponsorship of sporting events is no big deal, even if the products involved are in contradiction of the ethos being celebrated. We live with contradictions, meeting them at every crossroad where self-interest meets ethics. I wouldn't imagine the concept of morality, enshrined in ethics, to be embedded in the twisting helix of our being, seeing as it can vary with times and locations. Self-interest, on the other hand, as the extension or guardian of self-preservation, is a constant and a *sine qua non* of existence. It operates at levels from the reflex ducking at sudden noise to the need to excel in a chosen area and concern with social acceptance and ascendancy.

* * * * * * * * *

It's not, is it? … no, it can't be … not Wilf Scriggins. Not the firebrand, champion of the working class and scourge of the Bosses. For a moment it looked like him. Can't be though. Sitting chatting and joking with the industrialist Lord Epitome of Bossly? … Actually, it is. It's that we are not used to seeing him dressed in ermine. He's Lord Wilf of Somewhere North now.

* * * * * * * * *

Short of a natural or economic cataclysm laying waste its institutions, it would appear that Capitalism is here to stay. It operates on profit, as it must, and it's the engine for our progress and prosperity. Provided that adequate checks are kept on exploitation, abuse and excessive avarice, its benefits can be widely spread. Along with triple-glazing, central heating, refrigeration, sanitation, labour-saving appliances, piped entertainment and instant access to world-wide communication, it delivers the luxury of evaluating the ethics on which it operates.

It is largely fuelled by the vision, initiative, energy and single-mindedness of exceptional individuals with highly-developed instincts to succeed. These, like the killer instinct in sheepdogs, can be channelled to useful purpose.

We all operate, to varying degrees, on inducements bringing reward. Investments for returns, be it in achievement, gratification, knowledge or love. At its most fundamental level, it operates as safeguard for species survival in the means of procreation.

Yet, for all that, there is a sublime beauty made poignant by the awareness of its transience in our reaching out for that which … oh, Hell … I've gone past my stop … now I'll have to hoof it back half a mile … and of course … pissing down again … with a vengeance … bloody sodding buses … Oeffff.

Life at the Blunt Edge

.... and out of his mouth went a sharp two-edged sword.

" .... No, it's not what I meant. I was only using it to get to the point I'm trying to make. Don't get me wrong. I love TV. Me, I watch anything that moves, when I'm not dozing off in front of the set. In itself TV is a marvellous thing. You are snug in your armchair and there are all these images coming at you, virtually out of nowhere. I mean, the wireless is marvellous enough. Even if a particular programme isn't up to much, I enjoy the technical side. It's what I tell myself, anyway .... Not really. There was a time when I'd have liked to. I had this little wind-up Bolex cine camera and did a bit of filming. Mainly to do with the children when they were growing up. With the films now transferred on to CD, it's wonderful to be able to watch them with the children: themselves parents, some grandparents.

.... Yes, granted. Unlike me, you can be selective in your viewing. Perhaps restrict yourself to factual programmes, even exclusively to the news bulletins. You'd still be up against it .... What I'm trying to get to, if you give me a chance. You see, like all great inventions, TV can cut two ways, so to speak. Too much of a good thing.

Take the internal combustion engine. It has changed the way we live and the pace at which we live it. Directly and indirectly, we benefit from it and to a large extent are dependent on it. Such is the story of its success that there are areas of concentration where cars outnumber people.

As things are, we couldn't live without the car. Yet, if orthodox science is to be believed, neither can we live, or even exist in the long term, with the consequences of its emission. We can discount the prognosis as unduly alarmist if we wish, but we are still left with the desperate strife for acquisition and control of fuel sources; with the sanctions and strangle-holds from monopolies; with the justifications for military incursions under the veil of peace-keeping.

Talking of cars. The other day I was hoping to cross a road with an unending stream of nose-to-tail two-way traffic: small cars, big cars, vans, lorries, buses and great artics. Mesmerised into a reverie, I drifted to wondering what I might make of the assorted vehicles if coming upon them for the first time and without prior knowledge: say as a visiting extra-terrestrial. I might be forgiven for assuming that they were the inhabitants of the planet and on seeing beings disgorged from cars, buses or trains, take them to be the offspring of the inhabitants in a form of reproduction peculiar to the planet.

I'm here reminded of an incident which is not wholly unconnected at root and at the same time traces a familial disposition. We had rented our first TV set and on the first evening of its installing, the family sat agog at the box of wonders. In the course of the evening we were regaled by a vintage Cowboys-and-Indians film with the standard encircling of the covered wagons by the good guys and the baddies whooping round, evil of intent. With the circle eventually breached, both parties went at each other hammer and tongs and with considerable ensuing fatalities. Throughout the encounter, my Dad, bless him, had been showing signs of mounting agitation.

Reaching critical point, he let fly with a stunner: declaring that all those dead bodies piling up inside the set wouldn't do it any good and fearful that Radio Rentals would demand payment for a new set. Dear oh dear. Where are you, irony, when we need you? Who needs extra-terrestrials anyway? .... No, not a word of a lie, I do sadly assure you.

Where were we? Oh yes, selective viewing .... That's right. But for the sake of argument, let's say you restrict yourself to just the News. You are still up against it .... Well, you are. Remember that in the first place, reporting works on the principle that it is the one plane which crashes, not the thousands operating safely, that makes the News. So you see, even with the most scrupulous and objective reporting, were it to exist, you'd still be up against it. The very fact of focusing on an item isolates it from the flux of reality, with all its distractions and inter-relationships, thereby distorting truth. Then there's the presentation of the item, to say nothing of the manifold ways in which it can be received. However well-intentioned in wanting to make a go of it, Reality and Truth are by their nature incompatible ....

But not to the same extent. Then, if Joe Public wanted to keep up with what was happening in the world, he could of a Sunday morning pad along in his slippers to the corner Newsagent for the News of the World and pick up his Woodbines at the same time .... Yes, I know. Prided itself in the slogan that *all human life* was reflected in its pages .... Well, OK. *Pond life*. But the point is some positive effort was required on Joe's part and, of course, he could always get a different paper. That other reflector of life, the TV, safely ensconced in pretty well every home, can pump out its take on life round the clock, like it or lump it.

.... I realise that. It's never just the one thing. I just mentioned TV because its influence is pervasive. There's also the omniscient PC and the multi-tasking mobile phone, along with other technological miracles. All making their own demands. None *bad* in themselves. It's more that they tend to blunt our perception of everyday reality and the importance of personal interaction. It is now not unknown for two persons, both in the same room, to communicate via text messages.

Perhaps above all else, it's down to our psyche. You know, this tendency to turn anything on its head. To pull two ways. Who can blame us? Our very beings are compounded of two genders. And as anyone acquainted with the prevailing Christianity will know, good and evil are inherent in our nature.

Then there is the duality in speculations about our origin. In the red corner, analogous to tooth and claw: the Evolutionists. In the blue corner, with parity to the celestial: the Creationists. Confused? Of course we are. We always were. Now we are *Confused dot com*.

As an aside, I wonder what the official Evolutionist view is regarding the place of Homo Sapiens in the league table. Are we at a pinnacle or just at another anachronistic bump? After all, we haven't been here long. The Dinosaurs straddled geological time and must have thought they were kingpins and here to stay. Of course, we are much more advanced and have no need to sit twiddling our thumbs in anticipation of a cataclysm. By virtue of our advancement, we may be granted the signal honour of contributing to our own premature demise.

Creationists are more clear-sighted about destinies, able to see beyond temporal horizons. Rather than progress as a species, the emphasis centres on the individual. For some there is the prospect of rehabilitation in paradisal surroundings for eternity. With duality kicking in for one last time, there is an alternative stringent programme for persistent offenders.

How tiresome the certainties and specifics of religious doctrines with the claims of privileged revelation and implied exclusivity. How touchingly eloquent of our need, as self-aware creatures, to mitigate the spectre in the extinction of the self.

......................Me? Firmly on the fence and open to all possibilities. With the preferred option in the acceptance that in the same way that heavenly bodies of great mass extert pull on those of lesser mass, so, once unencumbered, our essence may be drawn towards *The* Essence. How's that for non-committal? ....OK, OK, just an aside. Nothing personal, no offence intended. Misplaced humour.

We are all up against it .... Yes, perhaps not so much those of our own generation. We have too much baggage, are too entrenched and too readily given to making unfavourable comparisons with the so-called good old days. You can't help worrying though, can you? Even if your children are into their fifties and pretty much settled into their lives, there are still the grandchildren and the great grandchildren. Perhaps it was always so. The old piling on their concerns on the young. Conversely, the young in each generation are obliged to jettison the relics of old thinking and attitudes. Never more so than now with the changes brought about by the galloping technology. Where we needed to be steadfast, they need to be adaptable .... Yes, but don't forget that from a fresh starting point and free of comparisons, they are better placed to accept and cope with the status quo.

.... No, I can't agree. I believe the greatest problem or the greatest challenge, if we are to be optimistic, lies in the increasing tendency, courtesy of the galloping technology, for life to be lived second-hand, as it were. Vicariously. In a virtual reality. The idea of something as opposed to the thing itself. Sentiment replacing emotion, if you like. As that gifted purveyor of pithy insights, one O. Wilde, put it: *a sentimentalist is simply one who desires to have the luxury of an emotion without paying for it.*

Look at the outpouring of public grief over the death of some popular icon. Is it grief or to be seen to be grieving, especially in the presence of the TV cameras? I wonder how many of the distraught, vying with each other in the sincerity of their grief, give the next door neighbour the time of day. And those carpets of floral tributes. Can't be doing the florists any harm.

Do you know, I once worked in a public institution where, in an unguarded moment, a chap of dubious character made an interesting disclosure. Apparently, he was kept on a sort of retainer by a Firm of local glaziers. His brief was to periodically venture out under the cover of darkness and put bricks through windows .... No, I didn't say that. You shouldn't put words in my mouth. I did not say that Interflora employs a stable of runners who at a moment's notice, place flowers at a spot receiving media attention and start the ball rolling.

I will say one thing though. I felt there was a ghoulish undertone in connection with a recent prominent case of a child disappearance. People in their hundreds turned up from far and wide to help in the search. Even with the pleas from the Police that they should not do so, as the search was being obstructed and any available evidence compromised. An overflowing of public-spirited compassion? *Reality-Check Alert.*

It may be that out of what might appear to be a period of confused transition a new thinking; a new morality, will in time emerge. Less bound by social conventions and institutions than driven by self-determination. Morality, in any event, is built on shifting sands, varying with epoch and locality and where principles clash with self-interest. For selfish we are. Not necessarily in a bad way (perhaps 'self-ly' could be a better word). We don't do much without inducements and rewards of one sort or another. Our appetites, variously presenting as aspirations, crave gratification. It's the way we are programmed. That thrust for assertiveness in all living matter, which we call Nature, relentless and inexorable, continues to operate under the epidermis of whatever the social or cultural changes. In its absence, chances are that early on in our ascendency, we might have been threatened by the predicament of the present day Giant Panda.

.... Well it's as it is and always has been. Our lives a brief flicker of existence in a Universe as indifferent as it is vast. In our little revolving outpost, caught in the headwind of species imperatives intertwined with individual psyche, struggling to find meaning and purpose .... But how can it be accepted, in human terms, that one child is tucked snuggly in a warm bed with a goodnight kiss and another, orphaned and abandoned, huddles on a hostile pavement; that one is provided with sustenance and the other scrabbles in a refuse dump.

King or beggar, irrespective of travel plans, we all get off at the same terminus. Naked of status and possession, our validation resting on having loved and been loved."

dot NOT com

In 1982, a vague notion which had long laid claims to head-space, sharpened into an idea.

Two years later, the culmination of that idea was played out on the playing field of a school in Essex.

On that day, a capricious gust of wind could have, literally and metaphorically, blown the whole caboodle to shreds and with it two years of work, planning and considerable expense. It could have visited embarrassment, to say the least, on numerous youngsters, an appreciable number of adults as well as several public institutions. Moreover, it could have left enough egg on my face for an omelette to feed the five thousand.

It is as difficult to determine the original form of an idea as it is easy to rationalise on it, once carried out. Seeing ideas as gift horses, I am always loathe to look them in the mouth. If they come at a certain level of compulsion, then such considerations as *it-can't-be-done; too-much-work; too-expensive; too-time-consuming; I've-got-too-much-on; I'm struggling-with-essentials* or *what-would-be-the point-of-it* … just don't get a look-in. Whereas by nature I would be incapable of shifting cut-price ice lollies in the Sahara, when ensnared by an idea, I am afflicted by a distortion in vision which gives mountains the appearance of mole-hills.

Likened to a kind of infection, the idea here paraded spread from the host to pockets in Grays and Chadwell-St Mary with isolated cases reported in Aveley; South Ockendon; Basildon; Billericay; Benfleet; Chelmsford; Corringham; Orsett and Hadleigh in Essex and others as far afield as the Metropolis itself.

In setting down this account, after twenty-eight years, of the project which followed on from the idea, I can indulge myself by re-living the experience without the anxiety which went with it.

Secure now in the common sense, sobriety and sense of extended self-preservation of the grey time, I can but marvel at the level of lunacy involved in attempting, let alone completing the venture.

It had been one of my intentions to involve, in some way, all the pupils and staff of Torells School as well as parents and the extended community. In particular, I had hoped that the 1982 First Year Intake might take their involvement as a memory through their school days and possibly beyond. Whether or not that end was achieved is not for me to say.

I had known that I would be leaving Torells and teaching on completion of the project. The storm clouds were gathering on another front. With a combination of exhaustion and anti-climax, I left

Torells in some turmoil and consequently not able to fully express my appreciation and gratitude to colleagues, pupils and others for all the support, co-operation, enthusiasm, good will and generosity of spirit for what must have appeared a very dubious venture.

I recall my nineteen years at Torells with affection and feel fortunate and privileged to have taught there at a time when teachers were entrusted with a certain measure of freedom and initiative.

* * * * * * * * *

There had been some work done in the Art Department in which Fourth Year pupils contributed individual sections to a large abstract design. Favourable reactions suggested the possibility of further work in that direction. Suitable subjects for a design proved to be a stumbling block. Allowing several hundred pupils to 'do their own thing' towards an overall design had its attractions. Perhaps more so for the teacher than for the pupils who at that stage of their development might better benefit from contributing towards something pre-determined and preferably figurative.

A well-known painting; a portrait of the Queen; a Pop Star; a Sports personality; the Moon landing and an underwater scene were among the many suggestions to be rejected. At one point the front runner was a photomontage of Mount Rushmore with the faces of senior staff superimposed on those of the American Presidents. It was dismissed as overly weighing to the facetious. The idea was shelved.

It re-emerged in the Spring of 1982: clear, confident, fully-formed and unblinking in the invigoration of the season. The perfect and obvious solution to the design problem. Black and white for greater impact … graphic … of local connection … incorporating type and photographs … the front page of the local Thurrock Gazette.

But how could the range of greys be reproduced with equivalent grey mixtures of paint with all the attendant problems of maintaining quality control in the quantity of paint needed to, hopefully, involve in excess of five hundred painters?

Simple.

No grey mixtures required at all. Only black paint.

For half-tone illustration in newspapers, magazines and books, the photograph intended for reproduction is screened into a system of minute individual dots. The printer uses only black ink. The eye blends the individual dots into the tones of the photograph.

Theoretically it would be possible to reproduce a larger version of a newspaper page, including half-tones and only using black paint.

The Project: to produce an exact dot-for-dot replica of a Thurrock Gazette front

page to the size of a football pitch.

Well, actually, the Project was only part of the idea.

Why not, while at it, also make a film recording the progress of the Project to its conclusion? It would be a way of opening up the Project to go beyond the Art Department and include, in some way or other, the whole school, staff, parents, public figures, officials, Primary School children, Tom Cobley and all. It was time to have a talk with Head of Physics Alan Trusler.

We discussed the idea of a film to run alongside the Project as he drove me home for the start of the Summer holiday. We had worked together before. In 1976 we made a feature-length film on a Sci-Fi theme called 'The Seedlings'. It was an ambitious effort in Super-8 with sound track and synchronised dialogue. My friend's expertise with sound recording equipment and his ability to enhance vision with sound were *sine qua non* for any film contemplated.

The demands in the making of 'The Seedlings' had forced a clash of egos and left us in a state of armed neutrality. As a scientist, Mr Trusler was able to bring to bear technical resources and intellect in fraught contrast to my own abdominal intuitive leaps in the dark. Time and our magnanimous dispositions had worked their magic and my colleague embraced the idea of a film with enthusiasm.

In the September, the outlines of the Project/Film were discussed with the Head teacher who, although innocent at the time about the extent of the undertaking, gave official blessing and unqualified support.

The idea was then presented to the Editor of the Thurrock Gazette who, whilst expressing interest and qualified support for the venture, conducted the interview with the guarded courtesy accorded to uncertified lunatics.

Two weeks later found the Gazette photographer setting up his tripod on the School's flat roof. Below, in the playing field were assembled the entire First Year Intake for 1982 and senior members of staff. At a given signal, the assembled looked up towards the camera and waved enthusiastically. The Nikon froze the moment.

In the course of several assemblies, the First Years were acquainted with details of the Project/ Film and accepted, in some bewilderment, that they had been waving at a helicopter almost two years into the future as part of the completion of the Project/Film.

The Gazette included a half-page photograph of the waving group in a mock paste-up of the front page dated two years ahead to 1984. At that stage, the dots making up the half-tones of the photograph were not discernible by the naked eye. A specialist Firm in London delivered a high quality enlargement of the front page from a 10" x 8" negative. The enlargement measured 9 feet by 6 feet. The average size of the dots could then be seen to be about 1mm across.

Running alongside the preparatory planning for the Project, many approaches were made to numerous sources for possible financial support towards cost of materials and also equipment

The entire First Year intake for 1982 with Staff, used in the Mock-up of the Gazette.

Thurrock Gazette

MAIN EDITION

The paper that gives you more for your money

Incorporating: CORRINGHAM & STANFORD RECORDER Telephone: GRAYS THURROCK 72293/4/5 TELE-ADS: 77121

No. 0001   May, 1984   Registered as a newspaper at the Post Office   15p

End in sight for school's mammoth venture

TORELLS 'DOT' PROJECT REACHES A CLIMAX

The project gets under way

ALL EYES are turned skyward to await the arrival of a helicopter which will mark the culmination of nearly two years' work for a Grays school.

The helicopter — with the Torells film crew and a Gazette photographer aboard — was used to film a Gazette front page made up of thousands of painted dots.

But, unlike the "real" newspaper, with a type area measuring 15 inches by 10 inches, the Torells effort stretched 180 feet one way and 270 feet the other!

The project, part of a film entitled Year of the Dot, was begun in 1982 when, through several processes, an identical page as this — only the true size — was broken down into the individual dots that make up the type.

Each dot was painted on to separate sheets of paper, each one appropriately shaded to match the actual mark.

Because of the technicalities of making the film, this project had to be the first tackled, and one fine day last year, the youngsters waited for the noise of the helicopter which would provide final evidence that the project had been a success.

Two days previously the grass on the playing field was cut so the ground would be as dry as possible.

The next day a willing band of helpers staked out guidelines and the mammoth task of pegging out 11,664 sheets of dotted paper began.

Each piece had to be in its appropriate place for the picture to emerge. Wire staples were used to keep the pages in place, each painted black or white according to its position. Finally, lengths of nylon fishing line were stretched across the rectangle.

At the first sound of the helicopter's approach, first-year pupils moved out on to the field and filming began. . . .

ABOVE: Man in charge of the project, Mr Joe Fiol (seated) goes through some of the material with Mr A. Trustler and some of the first-year pupils.

The Mock-Up of the front page of the Thurrock Gazette prepared two years ahead of the completion of the project.

for the making of the film. In that respect we were indebted to Eastern Arts Association and to members of the Art Inspectorate.

The first draft storyline for the Film, to be titled 'Year of the Dot', was written. The treatment was to be Documentary/Fiction. 'Documentary' in the sense that the Project would be recorded as it progressed to its conclusion. 'Fiction' insofar as a story would be woven into the circumstances of the venture. For that purpose a group of 26 First Years formed the fictitious Form 1(D). Dave Edwards, Head of PE, gallantly consented to be their Form teacher and my alter ego, fronting the Film, leaving me free for the actual filming. He was not required to involve in the Project itself and it is a testament to his empathy and commitment that he was able to front it with such authority.

In the arrogance of my innocence, I had envisaged the possibility of involvement across subjects. Perhaps to do with calculations of magnification relative to distance of viewing. I also felt there to be educational mileage in the analogy of a dot, as the most basic mark and the components of matter in achieving mass through proliferation. There were difficulties in accommodating such deviations from strict subject syllabuses. Approaches to the local College with similar intention delivered similar outcome.

There were instances when the idea and scope of the Project brought forth observations which, if anything, only fuelled determination. At the time, personal computers had begun the march to becoming essential for living. With it came the implication that any task requiring calculation, complexity, repetition or logistics to any degree was best undertaken, if not exclusively, via a keyboard.

Yeah, right.

* * * * * * * * *

The storyline for 'Year of the Dot'.

Staff meeting. Newly-appointed Art Teacher Dave Edwards (DE) equires re probability of school funds being available for Form project work. Open for general discussion. Conflicting views. No funding.

Form 1(D). Registration. DE brusque. Orders silent reading. Explains Project is off. Bell for lessons.

1(D) along corridors. Whispers. Huddles.

Break. Playing field. Teachers Alan Campbell and Charles Haskett suspicious of 1(D) in huddle. 1(D) disperse as AC and CH approach.

Several pupils at home. Breakfast. Food items into school bags. Sleeping bags sneaked out.

Dining room. Lunch. Speeded up action of pupils queuing and darting about. Contrast Staff table. Slow motion synchronised eating. More food secreted by 1(D).

Office. Head teacher Miss B Finch. CH enters. Reports First Year pupils barricaded on school flat roof. DE enters, explains. Pupils 1(D) protest re stopping of Form Project. BF contacts Education Officer, Governors, Community Police Liaison Officer. DE and CH placate anxious parents by phone.

School forecourt. BF meets parents arriving in cars. View of heads along roof parapet. Education Officer, Governors, Police arrive.

School gates locked. Friday.

Evening into night into dawn.

Scattered sleeping bags. 1(D) asleep.

Staffroom. Monday AM. Pin-up notice re incident. 2 days suspension.

Classroom 1(D). Registration. Wednesday. Dressing down by DE. Subdued 1(D). DE lays on irresponsible behaviour, personal disappointment. Two-days suspension. DE turns situation around. Calls 1(D)'s bluff. They've got their wish but are they up to the Project? Up to showing the rest of the school what 1(D) can do other than whine. Resounding 'Yessir'.

Thurrock Gazette Office. Grays. DE explains Project to Editor. Photographer called in.

School flat roof. Photographer with DE. Set up tripod. Below, assembled First Year Intake plus senior staff. On signal all wave upwards at the camera.

Form room 1(D). DE shows 1(D) mock-up of Thurrock Gazette front page with photo from the school roof.

School trip DE with 1(D). Minibus. Gazette works in Basildon.

DE explains Project to 1(D). Art Block.

School library. Writing up of Project in folders.

Art Block. 9⊠ x 6⊠ enlargement marked vertically and horizontally to give 11,664 sections. Print cut into strips along the length of the enlarged front page. Numbered on the back. Hung up.

Art Block. Packets of A1 paper opened. Sheets numbered to accord with sections on strips.

DE's bedroom. Epidiascope. Projection of strips onto wall. Drawing round individual dots.

Completed sheets rolled up.

Art Block. Sheets unrolled. Pupils select sheets. Painting of dots. Black paint.

Painted sheets drying on floor. Accumulation –

Cutaways: mixing paint; DE at home preparing sheets; pupils painting; papers drying; piling up; piles numbered.

Art Block. Gill Wragg. Liz Callaghan. Pupil mixing paint. Bucket. Sink.

Pupil has fantasy. Gill Wragg, Liz Callaghan as witches mixing brew. (snake, skull, frog, bat). DE ogre. Pupil with 12-foot brush painting gigantic dots. Dots come to life.

Art Block. Painting. Pupils see Dalmatian in field.

Dalmatian brought into Art Block. Dalmatian painted over to appear white. Filmed. Washed down to reveal natural dots. Released.

Art Block. Montage of dot patterns on sheets.

Hall. DE approaches Dance teacher Lesley London.

Dance sequence. Hall. Into field.

Art Block. Sheets of A1 taped in strips.

Rolling up strips.

DE counts scrolls.

Boys' Gym. Strips gummed into sections.

Taping.

Sections opened up. Reversed. Rolled up. Tied.

School Hall. Completed rolls stored.

School field. DE measuring staking out.

D-Day. Pupils carrying rolls onto field.

Rolls untied. First one in position. Unrolled. Secured.

Cutaways. Close-ups: unrolling: hammering: tying down.

School onto field.

Dancers prepare.

Helicopter approaches. Lands. Rises towards A13.

Helicopter hovers.

Dot size as seen through
a magnifying glass from
the newspaper page.

As seen by the naked eye
on the 9' x 6' enlargement
of the newspaper page.

First projected magnification
onto A6 (5⅞" x 4⅛")

Final magnification
onto A1 (33⅛" x 23⅜").

Individual painted sheets are taped together.
Rolled up.

At a staff meeting, newly-appointed Art Teacher Dave Edwards raises the possibility of using the Form Period for a class project. The Headteacher invites discussion.

Jerri Harrison (History) has misgivings about a class project working in the case of Fourth (and Fifth year Forms!
Bob Delderfield (English) fears the Form Period veering away from Pastoral intent and becoming just another subject. Chuckie Spiers (Remedial Studies) asks what the intended project involves.

'The Dot' explains D.E.
Rodney Powell (Maths) quips on the 'dolours' of the project.
General hilarity ensues.

D.E. informs his Form 1 (D) that the project is off. Dismissed as a joke.

First year Tutor and D.E. face a dilemma.

The disappointed 1 (D) stage a protest by spending the night on the school flat roof.

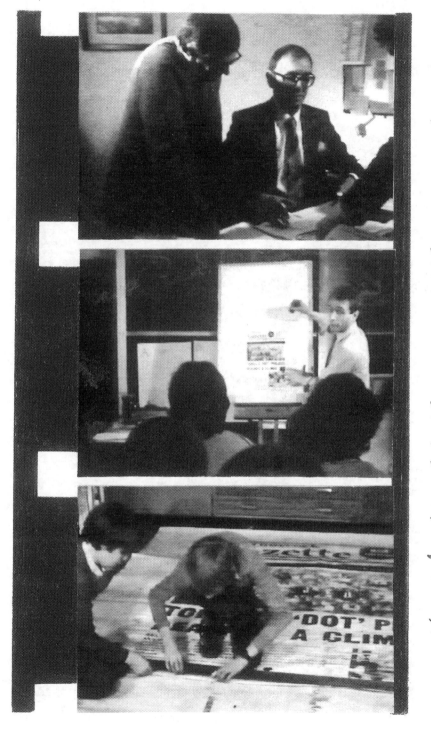

The project works. D.E. visits the office of the Thurrock Gazette. Discusses project with Terry Smith (Editor) and Dave Henderson (photographer).
A mock front page of the Gazette is drawn up post-dates two years. D.E. and 11(D) prepare by editing a 9"x6" enlargement into strips.

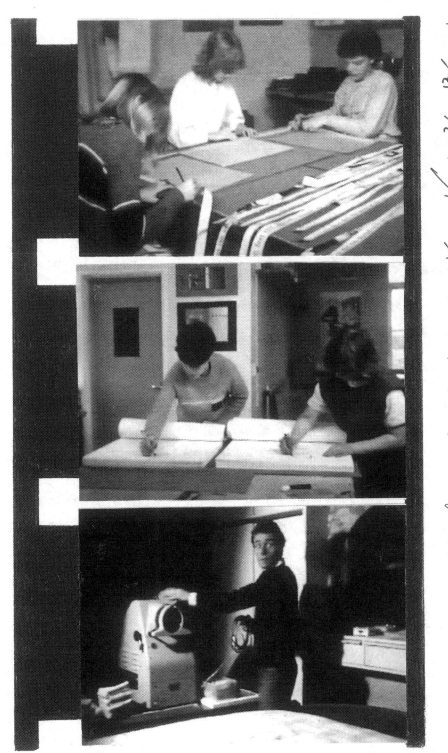

Strips are individual numbered, divided into sections 1⅜ x ¹³/₁₆ inches.

A1 Sheets are given corresponding numbers.

At home, D.E. I sets up the school epidiascope.

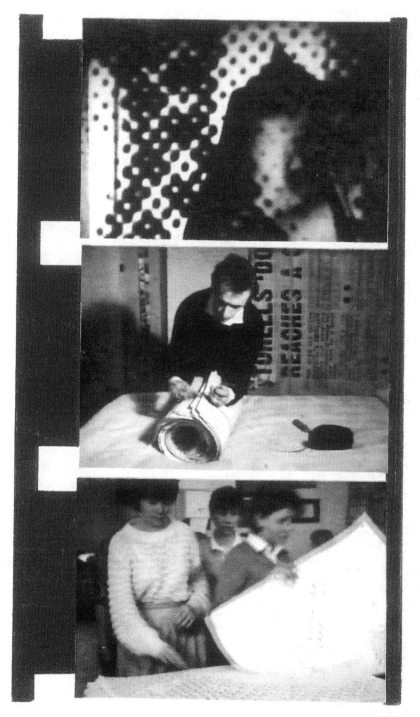

The laborious task of drawing round each individual dot, projected on to 11,664 sheets of A1, in two stages, begins. Completed sheets are rolled up. In the Art Block, pupils taken up the sheets.

painting begins.
Painted sheets laid out to dry.
D.E. stock takes

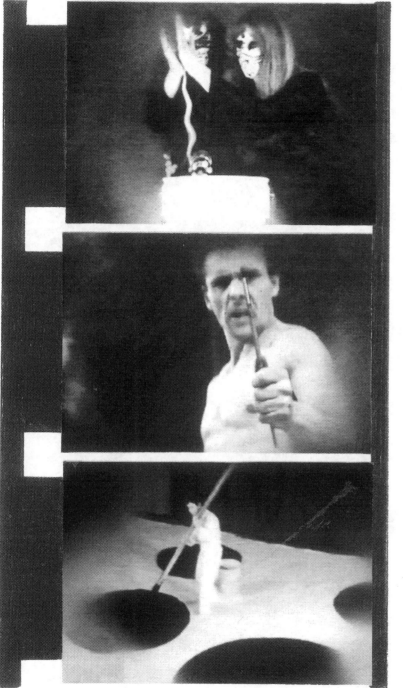

In the form of a pupil's reverie, Art Teachers/Witches Gill Wragg and Liz Vallaghant prepare a brew.

S.E./oone enforces painting.

Pupil complies.

In the Boys' Gym strips are taped in rolls of 12.

12 Runs 22 ft wide and 185 ft long rolled and stored.

D.E. Taking bearings.
Lesley London (dancer) planning for the aerial sequence involving dancers and Forms (one/two/three (years).

On 'D' day the rolls carried out of the school onto the Girls' Playing Field.

More rolls.

And yet more.

On the field
pegging out.
Complete.

One of three helicopters takes off.
View of the project by Dave Henderson (Thurrock Gazette).
Aerial sequences by 1st/2nd/3rd. years.

View of completed Project. Dancers into patterns.

Final spiral.

Art Block. DE + 1(D) looking at aerial photos.

DE called to assembly Hall.

Presented with Dalmatian pup.

Close-up. Pup.

* * * * * * * * *

The work proper on the 'Dot' Project could start.

The 9 feet x 6 feet enlargement of the Gazette front page was divided into a vertical/horizontal grid yielding 11,664 sections measuring $1\frac{1}{2}$ x $^{13}/_{16}$ inches. The print was then cut into strips along the length of the page. Each section was numbered on the reverse, starting with A1 for the first section on the first strip.

It was time for the master bedroom, by kind permission from the lady of the house, to undergo significant alterations which would hold true for the ensuing 18 months. With the furniture re-arranged, the School epidiascope was screwed into place on a solid table, itself secured to the floorboards at precisely 5.5x magnification from one bare wall. All impediments were removed to and from the one-eyed squatter, the door and the bed. Windows were permanently blacked out and dusting was made a capital offence.

Accuracy and registration were of the essence and best not attempted over a protracted period in the daily comings and goings of some 100 pupils in the Art Block.

The magnification to the final size needed to be done in two operations. The projection in one operation would require a distance which would weaken the resolution of the image.

The first strip was inserted into the epidiascope and the first section marked A1 projected on to the wall. The $1\frac{1}{2}$ x $^{13}/_{16}$ inches section onto a sheet of A6 paper measuring $6^{1}/_{16}$ x $4^{5}/_{16}$ inches, also marked A1. Registration strips of card for positioning of the subsequent 11,663 A6 sheets were glued onto the wall.

Then the penance began. A personal acquaintance with each separate individual blessed dot on the 11,664 A6 sheets.

There were problems in maintaining ink flow in the black markers held at the horizontal. After 30 dehydrated markers, black paint and sable brush took over to further complicate matters in the ambient gloom with spillage and stained fingers. Finally, black Conté pencil took over to encircle each separate individual blessed dot on the 11,664 sheets of A6 paper. *Amen.*

The operation complete, it was time to repeat the process. That time, the A6 sheets measuring $6^1/_{16}$ x $4^5/_{16}$ inches went into the epidiascope and projected onto A1 cartridge paper measuring $33^1/_8$ x $23\frac{1}{2}$ inches, giving the opportunity for personal re-acquaintance with each separate individual blessed dot on 11,664 sheets of A1 paper. *Deo gratias.*

A reasonable number of sheets with the outlined dots completed, the sheets were rolled up and taken to the school.

The painting of the dots began in earnest at Easter 1983. Black paint by the bucketful was dispensed into large jars and applied with brushes of various sizes. Each group coming into the Art Department painted for two sessions in each half term. Initially painting was confined to First Year pupils but, in time, extended to the Second Year and to non-exam groups in the Third and Fourth Years.

In addition, members of the Art Department visited Torells contributory schools, these being Chadwell, Herringham, Little Thurrock and Woodside Primary Schools to conduct painting sessions with Fourth Year Juniors. Pupils got into the spirit of the Project and the sessions developed a factory atmosphere, with painted sheets coming off fast and furious from conveyor belts, as pupils vied with each other to set up personal records.

A trolley was kept on permanent standby, fully equipped with sheets, paint, brushes, stirring sticks, water, buckets, powder paint, funnel, rags, empty jars. At a moment's notice it could be transported to any of the four working areas of the Art Department, or indeed, the School Hall.

A particular feature of this part of the Project was what became known as 'the black milk round'. This involved staff members driving around Chadwell and Grays at the start of school holidays delivering paper, brushes and black paint in milk bottles to pupils' homes. Pupils and families would get busy painting. It was not unusual to receive telephone calls from pupils, mums, dads or even grans on the evening of the morning delivery to say that their quota of sheets was finished and could they have some more. A special delivery would be made the following morning. This part of the operation coped with some 2,000 sheets.

While the painting continued relentlessly, the final screenplay was completed. Staff were approached regarding roles in the film. The technical equipment was made ready. A film crew made up from my Fourth Year non-exam Photography Group was set up. The film would have synchronous sound on a frame to pulse link between camera and recorder and shot in colour. The shooting script was prepared. Filming began in October 1983. From that point, it continued alongside the Project, recording activities as they took place and reconstructing those already completed.

By Easter 1984 the painting was completed. Of the 11,664 sheet No. AV22 was unaccounted for and replaced. Old solid wooden tables with inset inkwells were ferretted out of storerooms. A row of these 30 feet long became a permanent fixture in the Art Department.

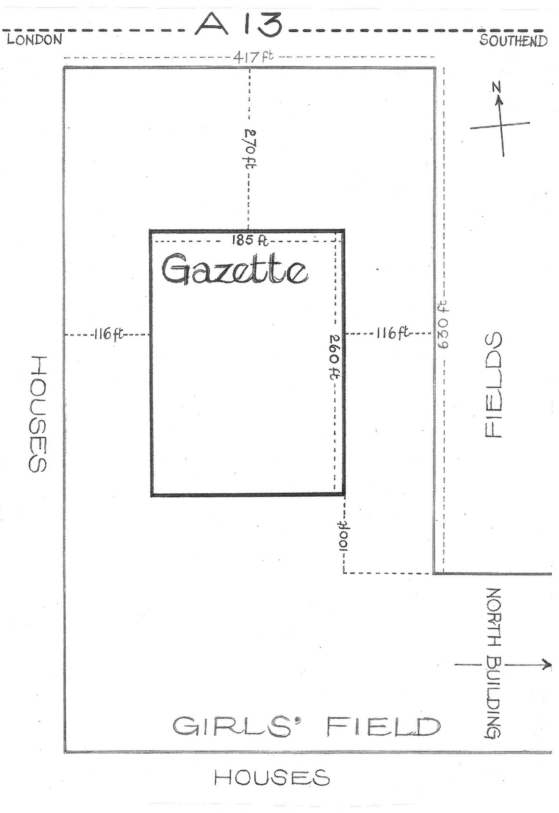

Pegging-out Plan

Sheets were laid face down on the tables and butt-joined with 2-inch gummed brown paper tape in runs of 33. 353 runs made up the front page. Next, on the floor of the Boys' Gym, the runs were taped together in groups of 8. The area of the Gym was filled 36 times with these sections. By 18th June, 12 rolls each 22 feet wide and 185 feet long lay tightly rolled in the Assembly Hall. There to await the day when they would lie flat on the field or scatter in shreds. The prognosis was not good. In a dummy run with 20 sheets taped together, a gust of wind had blown the sheets to the A13.

Laying terror aside, it was time to begin negotiations for a helicopter for a bird's eye view of the front page measuring 260 feet by 185 feet.

The Editor of the Gazette was invited to Torells to witness preparations. Confronted with the actuality, all reservations regarding the viability of the Project were withdrawn and the Gazette undertook to hire a helicopter for one afternoon.

A day had to be arranged which would meet the requirements of the school, the Gazette and also the B.B.C. and Thames Television, who had expressed interest in the Project.

The day was fixed for Wednesday 4th July 1984.

* * * * * * * * *

D-Day	The 4th July dawned with a light breeze and clear sky.
6.45am	Checked that the markers and string had held fast. Taking sightings from pylons and the College building on the previous evening an area had been marked out, hopefully giving a 90° angle at where the top and right sides of the front page met.
7.00am	The ubiquitous trolley rattled nervously towards the freshly-cut grass of the Girls' playing field. On board: 14 wooden mallets; 1,025 skewered pegs; 40 large steel pins; 500 4" nails; 1,500 cardboard reinforcers; 6 massive bobbins of string; 10 rolls of Sellotape; 14 pairs scissors; 4 hammers; black paint; brushes.
7.30am	Two teams made up of 3 teachers and 30 pupils each, took the first 4 rolls onto the field. The first roll was laid in position. Team A stood by.
8.00am	Team A went into action. The 'rollers' unrolled a section of roll No.1; the 'stretchers' stretched out any creases in the paper; the 'feeders' fed out ready-skewered cardboard reinforcers to the 'bangers'; these banged the reinforcers through the paper into the ground; the 'fixers' secured string across the surface of the paper. Under the vigilant eyes of the teachers, a further section was unrolled, keeping the edge of the paper in line with the pegged marking string. By the time roll No.1 was half-unrolled, Team B started on roll No.2. Team A would then start on roll

No.3 and so on for the 12 rolls. At the start of school, the remaining 8 rolls were taken out to the field.

While this was going on, the film crew were busy recording in sound and vision. Fourth Year pupil David Lewis took over the camera work, leaving me to float about in demented manner. David worked entirely on his own initiative.

The sky spawned dark clouds, the breeze freshened, sudden gusts threatened the work. It became crucial that at all times the paper was kept flat to the ground. A careless moment which allowed the wind to get under the paper would be disastrous. The wind kept changing direction, tearing at the paper against the pegs. The 'floaters' dashed around with extra reinforcement and making any tears good.

11.00am	The work hit a snag. The extra reinforcement needed to offset the wind depleted the stock. A despatch rider charged around the local hardware shops buying out stocks of 4 inch nails. Teams pressed on taking refreshment in relays.
12.30pm	The last roll laid out. By then the clouds looked ominous and sudden gusts continued to menace. The teams took their lunch in the field on standby duty. The slightest ripple under the sheets brought a blast from a whistle. All hands rushed to the danger spot, holding it down until the gust subsided or necessary repairs were carried out.
1.00pm	All staff, pupils, visitors and Press gathered on the field.
1.35pm	A particularly bad tear coincided with the staccato whirring of a helicopter approaching. The helicopter, chartered by the Thurrock Gazette, landed on the Boys' playing field. On board Gazette photographer Dave Henderson.
1.50pm	The helicopters carrying the BBC team from the Programme 'John Craven's Newsround' and ITV's 'Freetime' landed on the Boys' playing field.
2.00pm	The entire Third Year, the same pupils who in the First Year appeared on the photograph, were marshalled in readiness for the aerial sequence by teachers Lesley London, Deborah Brown and Pauline Bullock.
2.15pm	In relays, the 3 helicopters were airborne, rising and banking towards the A13. For reasons of safety David Lewis was not permitted to board. Instead, I accompanied Dave Henderson aboard the Gazette helicopter. At the A30, the three helicopters swerved to begin the approach. Altitude 500ft. Dave Henderson set the motorised Nikon going. I couldn't watch, my eyes tightly shut. Dave Henderson nudged me. I looked down. There it was. Startlingly legible. Impossibly perfect. Phew.
3.30pm	School was dismissed from the playing field.
5.00pm	An edited version of the day was re-lived on John Craven's Newsround.

Aerial view of the completed Project by Thurrock Gazette photographer David Henderson

Over the 1984 Summer holidays, a sequential edit reduced the footage from 9½ to 2 hours. Alternative takes were kept in case those selected were unacceptable soundwise.

In the September, the vision/sound editing began in earnest. Alan Trusler and I found a disused storeroom in the school where, to the consternation of the School Caretaker, we burned the midnight oil matching pulse to frame. We managed to complete the task three days before the film was due for its first showing at the Thameside Theatre in Grays in the November 1984.

For me there was an emotional and touching conclusion to the venture of the Project/Film. During one registration period, I was hoodwinked with a fake message from the Head to go to the Hall. There, with the assembled school, I was presented with a beautiful Dalmatian puppy.

* * * * * * * * *

Shopping List:

<u>Project</u>

11,700 sheets A6
11,700 sheets A1
50 rolls 2" gummed tape
2 Tape dispensers
40 gallons black powder paint
10 spare lamps. Epidiascope
10 rolls Sellotape
6/100 yds bobbins. String
10 packs A1 card
1,030 skewered pegs
40 large steel pins
500 4-inch nails
50 black markers
500 black Conté pencil

<u>Film</u>

Braun Nizo 801 super-8 camera
Blimp
Ball/socket tripod
Wheel dolly
1 Broadlite (2000W)
1 Blond (2000W)
2 Redheads (800W)
1 Flood (1500W)
Reflectors/Diffusers
60 yds extension cable
Uher 4000 Record Monitor Recorder
Reslo omnidirectional mic
AKG D900 Gun mic
Extension Boom
RS lapel mic
Elmo 912 Editor
Wurker splicer
Bauer T6 10 projector
Agfa PEM3656. Tape
Kodachrome 25 ASA Film
Duo-play splices

'Rollers', 'Stretchers', 'Feeders', 'Bangers', and 'Fixers' in action.

Vision and sound recording on 'D' Day.

Nearing Completion

Composed.

Decomposed.

Retouching damage.

Headteacher Miss B. Finch JP, 'bangs' the final peg.

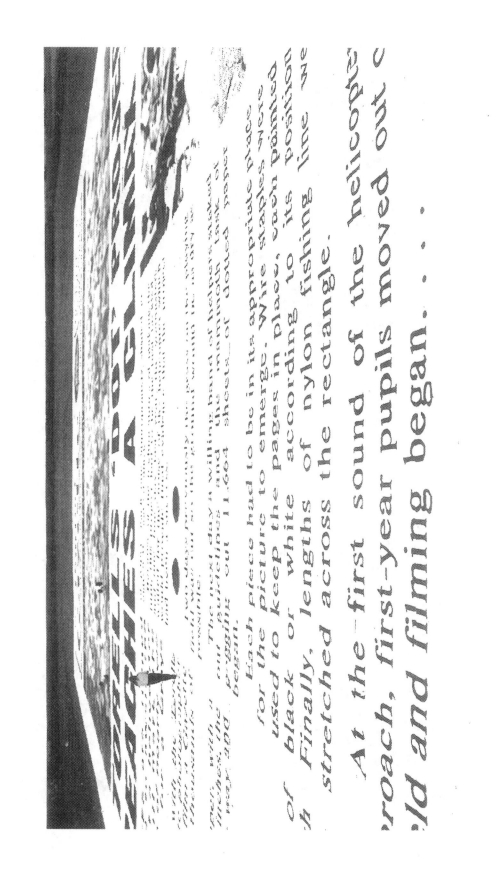

'Pegging out' Complete

The large expanses of glaring white were responsible for several reported cases of sunburn

A threatening gust

Filming for Thames TV "Freetime"

Interviews with pupils for the BBC Programme 'John Craven's Newsround'.

Interviews for BBC TV "John Craven's Newsround"

Recording for the BBC Programme 'John Craven's Newsround'.

Filming for BBC TV "John Craven's Newsround"

Dotty project heads for book of records

By David Henderson

THE Torells "DOT" project reached a thrilling climax last week when the massive special Thurrock Gazette front page was rolled out on to the school sports field.

The page, measuring 185 feet by 260 feet, took two years to plan and produce, was made up from 11,664 sheets of paper, and used almost 250 litres of paint. It showed how detailed pictures can be made up from millions of dots.

Pupils and staff started early on Wednesday morning, rolling out the huge rolls that were sections of the page.

Each section was carefully placed, and then pinned to the ground with special pegs to prevent the light breeze from lifting and damaging the paper.

Lines of light string crissed-crossed the whole page as extra protection against wind damage.

During the morning, the operation was filmed by a team from BBC television for John Craven's Newsround, and a crew from Thames television also recorded the event for Free Time, which will be transmitted later in the year.

Another camera team were also busy filming. The Torells crew were filming for the school's production The Year Of The Dot, a full 90-minute feature film which will be premiered at the Thameside Theatre towards the end of this year when editing has been completed.

The film and the Dot project was the brainchild of the school's art teacher, Mr Joe Fini, who was clearly concerned that the breeze would damage the page before filming was completed.

Early in the afternoon, a *Gazette* helicopter arrived from Southend and the giant page was filmed for the final sequences of the school film and for the record books.

Photographs and a copy of the *Thurrock Gazette* have been sent to Guiness Superlatives Limited, publishers of the Guiness Book of Records, in the hope that the Torells project will claim a place in their next edition for the largest newspaper page ever produced, a record that would be very hard to beat.

Thurrock Gazette — MAIN EDITION
The paper that gives you more for your money

End in sight for school's mammoth venture

TORELLS 'DOT' PROJECT REACHES A CLIMAX

The project gets under way

ALL EYES are turned skyward to await the arrival of a helicopter which will mark the culmination of nearly two years' work for a Grays school.

The helicopter — with the Torells film crew and a Gazette photographer aboard — was used to film a Gazette front page made up of thousands of painted dots.

But, unlike the "real" newspaper...

ABOVE: [caption illegible]

THIS giant page of the Thurrock Gazette looks so real that teams of pupils from Torells performed synchronised dancing around it when it was laid out in the school field last week — to prove on film that the page was real and that it wasn't just a photographer's trick.

The patterns made by the pupils will add scale to the mind-boggling page when seen on film from the air as part of the school's Year Of The Dot film, being produced at the school.

The page covered a soccer pitch and music was blasted over the field from powerful speakers so that the music could be heard above the noise of the helicopter.

Up front — your giant Gazette

THIS is the culmination of two years' work at Torells School, Grays — a front page of the *Thurrock Gazette* measuring 185ft by 260ft!

For the past two years children at the school have been working on reproducing a front page the size of a football pitch by means of special projection equipment. Gallons of paint and thousands of sheets of paper have been used, and on Wednesday the sheets, which had previously been joined into massive rolls, were staked out on the school field.

Our cameraman, David Henderson, had to take this shot from a helicopter to illustrate the magnitude of the project, the brainchild of Torells teacher Mr Joe Fiol.

record the event, and Mr Fiol used the helicopter, specially hired for the event by the *Gazette*.

Among those taking part on Wednesday were children from Liege, who were at the school as part of an exchange scheme. When the film of the Dot Project is completed it will be shown in Belgium,

THE TIMES
Educational Supplement

FRIDAY DECEMBER 7 1984   NUMBER 3571   FIRST PUBLISHED 1910   PRICE 50p

Big news . . . this giant front page of their local newspaper should get Torells Comprehensive School, Grays, Essex, into the *Guinness Book of Records*. The page, which measures 180 feet by 270 feet, covering the school's football pitch, was the culmination of a two-year project. It was the brainchild of Mr Joe Fiol, head of creative studies. The dots were painted on to 11,664 separate sheets of paper, stuck together and rolled out on to the grass for the benefit of the cameras.

Dot-to-dot

THE WESTMINSTER Press weekly paid-for, the *Thurrock Gazette*, received national television exposure with the aerial shot of a specially made-up front page measuring 185 ft. by 260 ft. featured on *UKPG* cover this week.

The paper joined forces with a local schoolteacher two years ago to produce an educational film called Year of the Dot.

Editor Terry Smith had a special tabloid page made up and, using projection techniques, pupils at Torells School in Grays reproduced each individual dot that makes up the page.

Nearly 12,000 separate sheets of paper were used and, prior to filming from the helicopter, these were joined into gigantic rolls.

On the day of filming, the rolls were joined to form the complete replica.

Said Mr. Smith: "When the teacher originally approached me about reproducing a page very nearly the size of a football pitch, I must admit I was apprehensive.

"Until the finished product was viewed from the air, there was no proof of success but having seen it, there can be no doubt.

"We are delighted to have been associated with the project particularly in this, our centenary year."

UK PRESS GAZETTE

JOURNALISM'S NEWSPAPER   No. 955   JULY 16, 1984   60p

The biggest splash in the world?

£113m. clinches deal for Mirror — p 5

WORKING ON the front can, as we all know, take a bit of time.

They've been working towards this particular page one of the weekly *Thurrock Gazette* for two years — all part of a project to produce an educational film. "Year of the Dot".

The other dots in the picture are people.

Dog explains all on page nine today.

UK PRESS GAZETTE

JOURNALISM'S NEWSPAPER   No. 978   DECEMBER 24/31, 1984   60p

How the papers made a splash in 1984 — page 8

Fatima's giant 'needle' points to the winners

THURROCK'S Olympic hope, Fatima Whitbread, was a surprise visitor to Torells School last week, to find the winners of the school lucky winners of a school lottery. The first two prizes were trips in a helicopter over Grays, and further cash prizes were also to be decided.

prize for a helicopter ride over the borough.

Fatima stood at the edge of the giant Gazette page and aimed her javelin to find the

Javelin champion Fatima stepped in at the last minute after it proved impossible to drop small parachutes from the helicopter filming the previous day. Four 'chutes were to have been dropped from the aircraft to find the winners, but the law prevented this!

Delighted pupils of Fatima's ex-school gathered around the page to watch the champion release her javelin, all hoping that she would prove a winner for them, and a winner for Britain in the Olympic Games next month.

Year of the Dot project on film gets first showing

ABOVE: The climax of Torells School dot project. After two years' painstaking work by pupils and staff, this giant front page was put together on a field and pictures were taken from a helicopter. Every aspect of the operation was filmed. (2784AU70)

RIGHT: Producer, director and head bottle washer, the schoolmaster who spent two years putting together the remarkable project, Joe Fiol, is applauded by an appreciative audience at the Thameside Theatre after the first-ever showing of the film. (4784AL9)

BELOW: Left, Mr Fiol with left to right managing director of John H. Burrows Mr Jim Banville, Thurrock Council chief executive Mr George Semaine, his wife Janet, head teacher of Torells Mrs Betty Finch and editor of the Gazette Mr Terry Smith. (4784AL92)

PREMIERE

THERE was a charged atmosphere at the Thameside Theatre, Grays, on Tuesday evening, for the world premiere of the Torells School film production, Year of the Dot.

The only thing that prevented the occasion being a glittering one was the lack of tiaras and royalty. Nevertheless, the evening had its own VIPs at the showing — the area education hierarchy!

Stars of the film were Torells form teacher Dave Edwards and the pupils of Form 1 (D). Mr Edwards played the starring role of Joe Fiol, the producer and director of the film, which told the story of the battle of Form 1 (D) to get the school to support its idea of a project based on the dot "the simplest form of mark we can make."

The project, the brainchild of Mr Fiol, took in all two years to complete and heavily involved the *Thurrock Gazette*. The climax of the film is a massive front page of the paper,

BELOW: Mrs Betty Finch, head teacher of Torells School, speaking after the showing of the film. (4784AL7)

measuring 260ft x 185ft, laid out on the school playing field.

The *Gazette* provided the helicopter for the aerial shots and dealt with the original page make-up.

By the time filming had been completed, there was enough footage for over nine hours' showing and it was necessary to condense this into 90 minutes. Mr Fiol and the man in charge of sound, Alan Trusler, spent many hours during the summer holidays in a cutting room at the school splicing the sequences together.

While Joe Fiol was in charge of filming, Alan Trusler was listening to dozens of records and making reels of sound effects for the production.

The result was stunning.

Year of the Dot may have been an educational film, but it did what many professional productions cannot do — hold the audience throughout. Not only was the music and sound superbly blended, the script showed originality.

With a story line that is not the strongest, it would have been easy to lapse into typical amateur footage of plenty of faces and sound.

Instead, the film took the audience through most of the emotions. It had seriousness, comedy, sadness, happiness . . . and the director had a keen eye for a good angle, too.

After the showing Mr Paul White, chairman of the County Education Committee, complimented the school and its staff and pupils on the production.

Head teacher Miss Betty Finch said her staff had shown tremendous support for the project and at times were working under considerable pressure. Without them all it would not have been possible to complete the film.

Following the showing of Year of the Dot, the editor of the *Thurrock Gazette*, Mr Terry Smith, announced that the paper was making a gift of £300 to Torells specifically for the purchase of computer equipment for pupils' use.

Together with some of the money raised at the sponsor afternoon held before half-term, the school would be buying a BBC Micro Model B.

Co-Producer of the Film, Alan Trusler, at the first showing of 'The Year of the Dot' at the Thameside Theatre, Grays, Essex.

SOUVENIR PROGRAMME

Thurrock **Gazette**

TORELLS 'DOT' PROJECT REACHES A CLIMAX

YEAR OF THE **DOT**

presented for its first showing
on TUESDAY, 20th NOVEMBER, 1984
at the THAMESIDE THEATRE, GRAYS, ESSEX
before an audience of distinguished guests
by **TORELLS COMPREHENSIVE SCHOOL**

PRELUDE
Selection of music used in the sound track

FILM

INTERMISSION
refreshments available at the bar

FILM (cont'd)

Councillor PAUL WHITE
Chairman, Education Committee

Mr. TERRY SMITH
Editor, Thurrock Gazette

Miss. BETTY FINCH, J.P.
Headteacher, Torells School

APPEARING IN THE FILM:

Form Teacher, 1(D) . . . . DAVE EDWARDS

Form 1(D) . . . . TRUDI ABLITT, DAWN ARCHER
SIMON BEVES, STEVEN BRIGHT
JANNA CARESWELL, JOHN CHANDLER
PAUL CLARK, MARK FAIRMAN, SIMON GEEN
CLAIRE GREEN, TRACEY HAMMETT
STEPHEN HARRINGTON, STEWART HENDERSON
LISA HILL, DARREN HILTON, BRYN HOOKER
DEAN MONKSFIELD, MATTHEW PAVELEY
JAMES RAY, SARAH STONE, SHEENA TELLING
DANNY VAUGHAN, TERESA WADHAMS, SARAH YATES

The Teachers . . . . ALAN BANNISTER, LIZ CALLAGHAN
ALAN CAMPBELL, BOB DELDERFIELD
STEVE ENTWISTLE, BETTY FINCH
MARK GIBBS, JEM HARRISON
CHARLES HASKETT, DEREK HOARE
MARK JOHNSON, CHRISTINA LEGRYS
JOHN NICHOLSON, MAUREEN NICHOLSON
RODNEY POWELL, BRIAN ROBINSON
CHRIS SPIERS, AL WATKINS, GILL WRAGG

The Parents . . . . JOHN & PAT ABLITT, MAVIS ARCHER
ALAN & LIZ BLAIR
KEITH & CAROL BRIGHT
JOHN & JOAN CHANDLER
CHRISTINE HAMMETT, MARGARET HENDERSON
JOAN HOOKER, JANET PAVELEY, PAMELA RAY
DAVID & MARY WADHAMS
PATRICK & GEORGINA YATES, JUDITH SALMON

The Officials . . . . PATRICIA GURNETT
RAY MORRIS, ALAN PALEY
WENDY WELHAM, PHIL NORTON

The Dancers . . . . SUZANNE BONES, JANNA CARESWELL
DONNA CRIDGE, ALISON DAVEY
NICOLA DICKENS, KELLIE DRUM, LISA FAGG
NICOLA HEMMINGS, TINA HOLDEN
JULIE MOON, PAULA SMITH, JACKIE SCHOFIELD
TERESA WADHAMS, JULIE WARRIOR
CAROLINE ZECHMEISTER

Choreography . . . . LESLEY LONDON

Thurrock Gazette . . . . TERRY SMITH, DAVE HENDERSON
GAZETTE STAFF at GRAYS & BASILDON

"Daniel" the Dalmation . . . . owned by JAMIE MAYO

Aerial Sequence . . . . TORELLS SECOND YEAR PUPILS

Directed by . . . . LESLEY LONDON
DEBORAH BROWN, PAULINE BULLOCK

The Helicopter used for the filming of the aerial shots
was provided by . . . . THE THURROCK GAZETTE

Stills . . . . CHRIS WILLIAMS, CHRIS SPIERS

Special Make-up . . . . DOREEN FIOL

Clapper . . . . DAVID HAINES

Lighting . . . . DAVID WATTS

Camera . . . . DAVID LEWIS

Production Assistant . . . . LYN WILSON

Sound . . . . ALAN TRUSLER

Written & Directed by . . . . JOSEPH FIOL

We acknowledge with gratitude the support and assistance given by: —
THE THURROCK GAZETTE in the general conduct of the 'DOT' Project.

MARGARET OGDEN, ROD PASSANT & MIKE CHALKLEY, members of the Inspectorate, with the provision of equipment and materials.

EASTERN ARTS ASSOCIATION with a grant towards the expenses of the project.

THE HEADTEACHERS, STAFF & PUPILS of CHADWELL, HERRINGHAM, LITTLE THURROCK & WOODSIDE PRIMARY SCHOOLS with the painting of the dots.

TONY SPIERS and STAFF with studio facilities at Thurrock Technical College.

DAVID TOBIAS from Visual Aids, Chelmsford with photographic material.

DAVE COOKE & TERRY BRADFORD of B.C.M. with facilities for post - production sound.

Screen presentation at the Thameside Theatre by

PETER MILTON

of

H. SPRINGETT & CO. LTD.

59 High Street, Maldon, Essex. (0621-52970)

specialists in Super-8 Movie Equipment

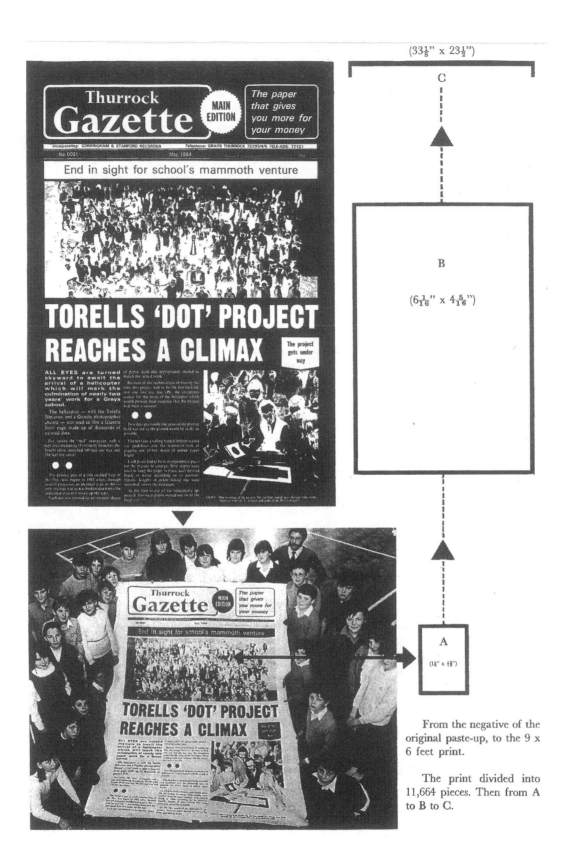

From the negative of the original paste-up, to the 9 x 6 feet print.

The print divided into 11,664 pieces. Then from A to B to C.

Film Crews from BBC and Thames Television record the occasion for the programmes: "John Craven's Newsround" and "Freetime".

...the first sound of the helicopter's a...
..., first-year pupils moved out on to t...
...d filming began. . . .

YEAR OF THE DOT

Joseph Fiol is head of creative studies at Torells Comprehensive School in Grays, Essex.

Here he tells us about a massive project he and many others have just completed.

It is a fact, perhaps a sad, significant or simply inevitable one, that today's youngsters see many more films than they read books. It is also a fact that in schools, our considerable efforts towards literacy are in no way balanced by even a recognition of the language of film.

True, art departments are served with a vague mandate to foster 'visual awareness' but this could be interpreted with equal justification as a concern for the urban environment or the tasteful selection of soft furnishings for the home. True again, there are spates of film-appreciation groups where films are either dissected or embalmed by discussion. Or, on a more practical level, 4(D) might take a video camera out to the playground and instantly record the inevitable bundle. Although both activities are connected with film making, the link is of the same tenuous nature as that between painting by numbers and art.

STRESSFUL

True, the making of a film of any length or involvement is a stressful and committing activity, and one not easily accommodated in a school timetable. BUT: fill a school hall with some 900 pupils from 11 to 16; be among them as they sit enthralled through a 90 minute film; witness their responses as they see themselves, their friends, teachers, classrooms, dining hall threaded into a story on a 10 x 7 ½ foot screen, and you are forced to concede that film-making — as opposed to the making of films as visual aids — can reach them in a special way.

Working in a comprehensive school, it has always been a matter of overriding personal concern that any film or project undertaken should involve as many pupils, teachers and members of the immediate community as possible. Our present film, *Year of the Dot*, actively involved some 500 pupils (many others less directly), the majority of the teaching staff, ancillary staff, parents, the Area Education Officer, school governors, inspectors, local police officers, the editorial and works staff of the local newspaper — plus two Dalmations, five frogs and one fish. From the outset the film was inextricably linked

Joseph Fiol plans a shot during the making of *Year of the Dot*

to a school project. Not least of our considerations was sustaining the impetus of film and project over a period of two years.

FAVOURABLE

In 1980, a piece of work had been caried out in the Art Department in which pupils contributed individual sections to a large abstract design. Favourable reactions had left a vague desire to develop the idea. In July 1982, the tangible form of the project was arrived at.

It involved, in the first instance, co-operation with the local *Thurrock Gazette* in producing a paste-up of their front page to our specifications. It included a half page photograph of our entire first year intake, together with teaching staff, waving skyward. The page was dated 1984.

The paste-up was photographed and enlarged commercially to a high quality print measuring 9 x 6 feet. At that magnification, the dots that make up the grey tones of the photograph were clearly identifiable. Next, the print was divided into a horizontal-/vertical grid of 11,664 sections, each 1 ⅛ x 5 5/16 inches. These sheets were then, in turn, projected and the image, whether dots or areas of print, was outlined in pencil onto a sheet of paper 6 1/6 x 4 15/16 inches. These sheets were then in turn projected, and again the images outlined, using thick black felt-tip pens, onto A1 Car-

tridge paper, 33 ⅛ x 23 ½ inches. The dots or areas on the 11,664 sheets of cartridge paper were filled in using black paint — some 40 gallons of it. Over 1 ½ miles of 2 inch brown gummed paper tape were then used to butt-join the sheets on the reverse side in runs of 33, according to the horizontal order of the original grid. The runs totalled 353. Finally the runs were taped into 12 rolled sections, each 22 feet wide and 185 feet long.

COMPLETION

The climax and completion of the project came on July 4 1984. It was then that the Torell's edition of the *Thurrock Gazette*, now measuring 260 x 185 feet, was pegged out on the school playing field in the face of a threatening, capricious wind. At an altitude of some 500 feet, from a helicopter chartered by the *Thurrock Gazette*, the front page was legible to the cameras of the BBC's *John Craven's Newsround*, Thames TV's *Freetime*, the *Gazette* photographer and Torrell's film crew.

Preparation for *Year Of The Dot* began with the treatment — which was fiction documentary. The conduct of the project provided the documentary aspect which was set in a probable, but strictly speaking, fictious, school background. A first-draft storyline was circulated to all staff and the feedback was considered in the final draft. A screenplay

MINIMUM

Filming began in October 1983 with the dialogue scenes, starting with a full staff meeting in session. Rehearsals were kept to a minimum with actors, and usually took the form of a run-through on the day before the actual shot. Technical rehearsals were always more involved, and covered the availability of power plants, lighting requirements, sound ambience and camera angles and movements. The construction of an efficient blimp eliminated the problem of camera noise.

Each location brought its own problems. One of the more extreme solutions was to have a pupil hugging a ceiling girder to minimise the reverberation of sound in a confined locations. Lighting, always inadequate for the amateur, necessitated some hard decisions in regard to the choice of natural, artificial or mixed lighting. Does one shoot for daylight at 25 ASA and cope with the harsh shadows? What do you do if your exposure will never budge from f/1.8 no matter what you do?

SEPARATELY

After the dialogue scenes, we shot the special effects scenes. They followed the 'working scenes' of the project. These were largely shot with unblimped camera with sound recorded separately. The earlier states of the project, which had been completed before filming began, had to be reconstructed until a point was reached when the work on the project could be filmed as it took place.

The climax of the filming came, as for the project, on July 4 — a 'live' strictly 'one-off' occasion. Considerable planning was required to make sure that all the aspects of vision and sound as set out in the storyline were covered both on the ground and from the air. An additional feature to be covered was the actual filming of the entire third year — those same kids who had posed for the photographer in their first year — doing a movement routine. By gracious permission of the threatening capricious wind, all aspects of the assignment were covered. 36 rolls of film were exposed.

ALTERNATIVE

Over the summer holidays, a sequential edit on the vision reduced the footage from 9½ hours to two hours. Alternative takes were kept in a case those selected were unacceptable soundwise. In September 1984 vision/sound editing began in earnest. We used the Elmo 912 editor with frame counter in combination with the Farnell-Tandberg for our last film *The Seedlings* in 1976. We still use it in preference to other systems on the market. Our Uher recorder, although admirable for recording, proved a little

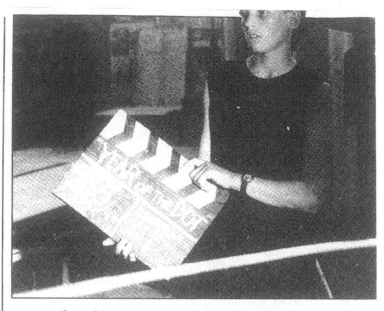

Scene 35, and the clapper boy still looks eager and willing

less of a versatile editing machine than the Tandberg. Temporary Sellotape splices were used in the course of editing. Final splicing was done on the superb Wurker splicer, using Duoplay splices. We used the Bauer T610 projector fitted with a pulse generator by REM Electronic for the laying of the soundtrack.

The use of music plays an important part in the setting of mood and pace as well as in the enhancement of the visuals. It came into consideration when planning the treatment. Certain passages in the film were conceived and cut to the music. One such passage was a dance sequence choreographed to take place in different locations. We were able to keep the flow of movement from location to location as well as show different angles of the dance by playing the music with a numbered guide track. We then used these numbers as locating points when editing.

CONSUMPTION

After a heavy consumption of midnight oil, the film, finally reduced t just under 90 minutes, was ready thre days before its scheduled premiere a the Thameside Theatre, Grays, o November 20 1984 before an invite audience.

A special effort was made early o the planning of the production to en sure that at least the first showin would be presented under optimun conditions. The facilities and services of the Thameside Theatre, together with the projection of Peter Milton of Springetts Ltd. on his Elmo Xenon, fully met these conditions.

The film had an excellent reception. It has had seven subsequent showings in our school hall. At the time of writing it goes into a period of enforced rest in readiness for entry into the IAC and *Movie Maker* competitions, 1985. ∎

Filming is a serious business, as witnessed by one of the cameramen
on *Year of the Dot*

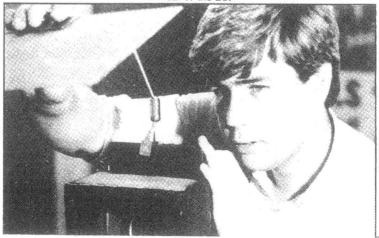

Out of the Mouths of Babes

You are too this, too involved with that or else with not enough or too much of the other. You turn round and your children are no longer children.

You get to remembering. Things they said. But it's like with jokes. Funny but you can't always remember them to tell.

Our own children started talking at an early age. Of the seven, no two turned out alike, although they all came with a similar take on life. Sometimes at odds with the general run.

You get to regretting. A wasted emotion. Time has moved on. Better to make amends where possible. In any case as a general rule the male, unlike the female, needs to grow up himself before he can appreciate the disarming candour of the very young.

Luckily, Mum Nature wisely invented the extended family, giving the retarded male a second chance with grandchildren. Then when you are no longer this or involved with that and with not too little or too much of the other, you are better placed.

So. I got to pestering my girls, themselves parents and grandparents and fully, in their turn, caught up in the whirl of this, that and the other. Got them to come up with things their little ones have said before they become like the jokes you can't quite remember.

The sample here given comes from the time that the children were of Primary School age. Only sixteen of the seventeen grandchildren are quoted. This is because the seventeenth, Phoebe, is a late arrival with already grown-up siblings and more of an age of the next generation of great grandchildren headed by Rhys, Isabel, Jude and Nolan.

In this selection of little gems from pearly teeth, some of the quoted have rather a lot to say. Others rely more on mannerisms, gestures and attitudes to make their presence felt.

* * * * * *

With her abundance of luxurious black hair, Ava has been told that she looks like the singer Diana Ross. She is on a visit to the Natural History Museum with mother and they go into the Prehistory Section. Ava points to the assembled remains of Tyrannasorous Rex:

"Look, Mum. A Diana Ross."

* * *

Ben has discovered the idea of numbers. However, when counting, he does not do so sequentially. If counting, say six apples, he will point to each in turn saying 'one apple', 'one apple' six times. An angelic-looking child with curly hair and big brown eyes, he is sitting on the wall of his grandparents' garden, which overlooks a bend in the country road. Several cars approach slowly. As they draw level with the wall, the little angel counts aloud:

"One car, one car, one car." The leading Sports Coupé swerves slightly.

* * *

Having arrived at a considered conclusion, Alice makes the announcement:

"I know the difference between grown-ups and children.

Grown-ups swear and make babies. Children don't."

* * *

Mother is feeding the new baby. Danny looks on with a look of disapproval. He has not long started putting words together.

"Baby down go kitch cook," he manages to say.

* * *

Sam is enthralled watching an episode of the TV programme 'Casualty'. In it a medical team is clustered around a patient's bed administering in due dramatic fashion.

"You seem very interested Sam. Would you like to be one of the doctors?" asks mother fondly.

"No. The patient," corrects Sam, eyes glued to the set.

* * *

By the look on his face, it seems Wayne has cracked it.

"I know what I am. I am a fuming bean."

* * *

The Good Friday service is long, the congregation repeatedly standing, kneeling and sitting. Fran is bored, fed up and fidgeting.

"Darling," whispers mother. "Try and pay attention, there's a good girl. Think of poor Jesus. How He must feel nailed to the Cross."

"He doesn't have to be up down up down all the time," frowns Fran.

* * *

Georgia's and grandfather's birthdays fall within a day of each other's.

"So what did you get, George?" enquires GF. Georgia trots out a list which includes the CD 'That's what I call Music 77'.

"Some of us got a CD of proper music," says GF deprecatingly.

"Not more bloody opera", counters Georgia snortingly.

* * *

Mother overhears Natasha describe someone as a 'plum'.

"What's a 'plum' love?" enquires mother. Apparently at a loss to explain, Natasha looks around the room.

"Her a plum", she elucidates, pointing at her aunt, who has been looking after her for some time.

* * *

Mother is insistent that on the way to the park, the older children keep hold of the baby's pushchair. Once there, she tells them:

"Right. You can let go now. Sod off and play."

Mother is telling the children about a coming holiday at Butlins. Ricky is beside himself with excitement.

"Mum, mum. Is it a place where we can sod off?" he blurts out.

* * *

At Parents' Evening, mother is told what an asset and general help Nikita is for her Class Teacher. At home mother compliments Nikita.

"Mum. I tell them every time. Don't scrape your chairs. Just lift them. But will they listen." Says Nikita with exasperated tone and gesture.

* * *

Carmen is telling a story:

"There was this little girl but she was really a princess. One day, she went to the park and went up on the slide and then a wicked witch came up behind her and, you know what? … she was bloody ugly …"

* * *

"Mum," complains Bianca coming into the kitchen. "Will you please do something about Simba. He keeps shagging my leg."

* * *

Alice is sitting at the dining room table engrossed in paint, water, brush and paper.

"Try and keep the paint to that side of the table, won't you darling," says mother on her way to the kitchen. Returning later, mother is dismayed.

"Oh, Alice. Look at the mess. Paint all over the table. Oh and on your chair and look, even on the floor." The artist looks up unabashed.

"I do need a studio, you know," she states in mitigation.

* * *

As a child, Danny suffered from asthma, which he has outgrown. During a particularly distressing episode, mother thinks it best to call for an ambulance.

"Won't be long now darling. The ambulance is on its way. Try and relax. Can I get you anything?"

"Sausage, beans and chips" says Danny between gasps.

* * *

Grandmother is visiting. In the car, going home from the train station, Ava asks:

"Nana, what happens to your bones when you die? Do they put them in a box and bury them in the ground?"

"Why do you ask, love?" says GM.

"Well, I don't want them to put all your bones in a box. I would like to keep some."

"Ah, would you, my darling?"

"Yes. Then I could play with them and make patterns."

* * *

Cooing, the family is gathered around baby Georgia, the first mixed-race addition. Ben hovers at the edge of the group, looking on. After some time, he shakes his head and, with hands in pockets, walks away muttering:

"Is that a white skin … I don't think so."

* * *

A family quiz is in progress. Ricky looks glummer by the minute as the others pipe up with ready answers. Comes the question 'Who built the Ark?' Ricky comes to life:

"I know the answer, I know the answer. It was no one."

* * *

Grandfather is showing a group of his grandchildren around his latest Art Exhibition. The children appear impressed: *did you paint all the pictures/is it very hard/how long did this one take/ what kind of paint is this/how did you get the big ones through the door/what's this one supposed to be.* GF notices Alice standing alone in the doorway to the gallery and goes over to her.

"Are you OK, Alice?" Alice shakes her head slowly, looks across the gallery and holds out both palms.

"But Papa. Why?" she asks in a tone of sympathy.

* * *

Ava has won the £10 prize in a Painting Competition held by the local library.

"So," ask the proud parents. "Do you know what you are going to do with the prize money?"

"Yes. I'm going to spend it all."

"Oh, are you? Do you know what on?"

"Yes. I'm going to buy a willie."

"Are you, love? That's … interesting. And where are you going to buy one? Do you know?"

"IKEA."

* * *

Mother is concerned that Wayne appears inclined to gentle ways, rather than the rough-and-tumble normally associated with boys. She is somewhat reassured when Wayne boasts one day that if ever a burglar came into the house he (Wayne) would kill him.

"Ah, you'd do that to protect mummy, would you, love?"

"Yes. I'd shoot him dead … with a pink gun."

* * *

Fran and big sister Chlöe are staying at cousin Wayne's house on a short visit. At bedtime they are shown the sleeping arrangements.

"Here we are," says Aunt. "A single bed and a double bunk bed. I'll leave you to sort out where you want to sleep. Only, Wayne always likes to sleep on the top bunk." The aunt leaves and a squabble between the sisters starts, as each is determined to occupy the bottom bunk. Fran feels she is losing ground.

"But Chlöe," she pleads is sweet exasperation. "You know I can only sleep with boys who wear glasses."

* * *

In the hushed reverence of the Consecration at Mass, the Sanctus bell rings.

"Phone," pipes up Sam.

* * *

Trapped in truculent mood, Ava throws the TV remote control at mother.

"Ava, you do not do that," admonishes mother. "Now then, young lady, what do you say?"

"Catch," says Ava.

* * *

Grandmother, on a visit, is chatting to Ben.

"So, what's your favourite dinner, Ben?"

"Sausages and chips."

"Mm. Do you have it very often?"

"Yes."

"So when was the last time you had sausages and chips?"

"Yesterday."

"I bet you enjoyed it."

"No."

"Oh, why was that? I thought it was your favourite."

"It is but there was pepper on the chips."

"Oh dear. It spoiled it for you."

"No. I licked off the pepper and then I ate the chips."

* * *

Teacher is talking about 'feelings' with the class: what they are/how they show/how they affect etc.

"Now then. Can anyone name any of these feelings we have?"

"Joy, Miss."

"Good. Any other?"

"Happiness, Miss."

"Yeees. That's like joy, isn't it? Any other?"

"Love, Miss."

"Yes, very good. Any more? Anyone? What about you, Ava?" Ava holds out one hand with fingers bunched. Extending one finger at a time, she obliges:

"Humiliation … disgust … bor …"

"Yes. Thank you, Ava."

* * *

Humming contentedly to herself, mother is breast-feeding Carmen. Carmen stops feeding and glares at mother.

"Shush," she says and continues feeding.

* * *

At her grandparents' house, Georgia is asked to fetch the milk from the fridge. Opening the fridge door, she is assailed by the odour of left-over vegetables.

"What a stink-bomb," she exclaims, quickly shutting the door.

* * *

Studying herself at some length in the mirror, Carmen frowns and slowly nods her head.

"Ava is right. I do have a big head," she concedes.

* * *

The family are gathered around the baptismal font. The priest approaches, clad in his vestments.

"Mu-um, look," whispers Danny in awe. "It's Jesus."

* * *

The young new teacher asks the children their first names in turn. He tells them his first name is Matt. At home, Ava is asked:

"Well, how did you get on with your new teacher?"

"Alright."

"Well, is she nice?"

"It's not a 'she'. It's a 'he'."

"Oh, so what's his name then?"

"Umm … er … carpet … or something." said dismissively.

* * *

The school play is on a Biblical theme with the stentorian unseen voice of Jehovah intermittently sounding from above.

"Good play, was it, Sam?" asks father at home.

"Yes," says Sam. "But I didn't like the baddie shouting all the time."

* * *

"Mummy, I'm the star in the school play," proudly announces Carmen.

"No, darling," says mother kindly. "There are no stars in the school play. All the parts the children play are important."

"But, Mum," insists Carmen. "When I go on the stage, the Angel says 'follow the star'".

"That's a different kind of star, love."

"But mummy, look." Carmen gives mother a copy of the programme. The cover shows a photo of the cast, among them Carmen in a white costume with huge pointy bits sticking out.

* * *

Carmen has contracted a stomach bug and is giving it due dramatic concern.

"Mum, I have a pain. It's in my tummy and in my head and everywhere as well. Oh it does hurt.

"Give her a pain-killer, mum, " suggests Ava.

"No, Ava. I can't give her a pain-killer. It's a bug" says Mum.

"It's a pain," says Carmen emphatically. "Kill it."

* * *

"We are going to decorate your bedroom, Carmen. How would you like it to look, do you know?"

"I do know. I would like blue walls, green curtains and a red carpet."

"We don't think a red carpet would be a good idea. You see, it wouldn't go with the colour scheme."

Carmen is telling a friend about her new bedroom.

"I'm going to have blue walls and green curtains. But I can't have a red carpet because it doesn't go with my colour skin."

* * *

"I bet you can't do this," says grandfather, balancing on one leg with arms folded. Zöe is in belligerent, competitive mood.

"I can so" retorts Zöe and follows suite.

"Yeah but I bet you can't do this," says GF this time holding one knee high with one hand, the other hand on top of the head and hopping forward and backwards. With some difficulty and grim determination, Zöe accomplishes the feat. Several other challenges are laid down and met in a committed manner.

"Ah, but," taunts GF. "If I wanted to, I could put one arm behind my back and then I could reach up and up until I could touch my head. You couldn't do that, ha ha." Hands on hips, head thrust forward and a defiant smirk on her face, Zöe says:

"I'd get a ladder."

* * * * *

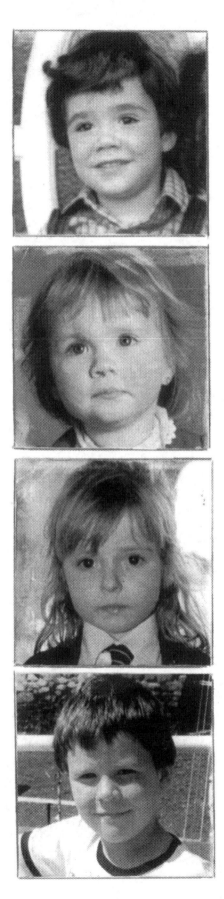

Daniel (b. 13/5/1981)

Zoe (b. 3-6-1983)

Natasha (b. 24/1/1984)

Richard (b. 9/5/1986)

Wayne (b. 22/10/1986)

Samuel (b. 1/10/1989)

Nikita (b. 19/11/1989)

Chloe (b. 22/11/1989)

Bianca (b. 24/1/1991)

Francesca (b. 4/4/1991)

Connor (b. 16/1/1992)

Benjamin (b. 6/6/1993)

Alice (b. 13/12/1993)

Georgia (b. 18/3/1998)

Ava (b. 21/8/2000)

Carmen (b. 12/9/2006)

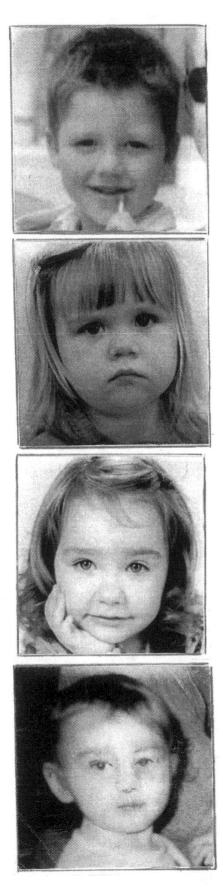

Rhys (b. 28/11/2007)

Isabel (b. 29/3/2010)

Phoebe (b. 6/4/2010)

Jude (b. 3/4/2011)

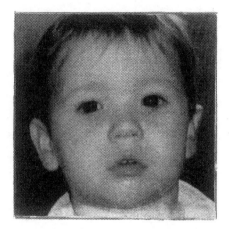

Nolan (b. 11/11/2011).